CW00919646

The Time Management Memory Jogger™

Create Time for the Life You Want

Peggy Duncan

First Edition | GOAL/QPC

The Time Management Memory Jogger™

Development Team
 Peggy Duncan, *Author*
 nSight, Inc., *Project Editing*
 Susan Griebel, *Project Leader*
 Janet MacCausland, *Cover & Book Design*

GOAL/QPC
12 Manor Parkway, Salem, NH 03079-2862
Toll free: **800.643.4316** or 603.893.1944
Fax: 603.870.9122
E-mail: service@goalqpc.com
www.MemoryJogger.com

Printed in the United States of America

First Edition
10 9 8 7 6 5 4 3 2 1

ISBN: 978-1-57681-106-1

About the Author

 Peggy Duncan is a personal productivity consultant and workshop leader. She travels internationally providing training and consulting to various levels of management and administration on organization; time management; and technology tips, tricks, and strategies in Microsoft® Word, Excel®, PowerPoint®, and Outlook®. She examines every aspect of how her clients work and helps them develop faster, smarter ways to get it done.

Duncan was formally trained at IBM. She was a project manager there when she was recognized by the chairman for streamlining processes that saved the company close to a million dollars a year.

Duncan is also a technology blogger and author of "Conquer Email Overload with Better Habits, Etiquette, and Outlook" and also "Just Show Me Which Button to Click! in PowerPoint." She has appeared on the TODAY show, ABC News, PBS, and Black Enterprise Business Report. Her expertise has been cited in O-*The Oprah Magazine, Entrepreneur, Real Simple, Health, Fitness, Black Enterprise, Self, Good Housekeeping, PINK, Positive Thinking, Men's Health, The New York Times, The Wall Street Journal,* and *The International Herald Tribune.*

The Durham, North Carolina native received a BBA degree in marketing and a train-the-trainer certification from Georgia State University. Currently living in Atlanta, Georgia, she travels widely to spread the word about time management.

About this Book

The methods outlined in this book are designed to save you more than just a minute here and there. You will save hours or even days if you spend time up front—now—to make the necessary changes to how you are currently working. Some of the forms in this book are available as free downloads on the author's page on our web site at:

www.MemoryJogger.com/peggyduncan

Acknowledgements

A sincere thank-you goes to our reviewers whose helpful suggestions ensured that *The Time Management Memory Jogger*™ would appeal to a variety of readers. Thank-you to my family who understands that writing projects can tuck me away for months and make me forget about anything else. I appreciate you so much for constantly reminding me to exercise and drink water.

Congratulations to all of you who will put the principles throughout this book to work and start to create time for the good life.

Our reviewer panel:
   Lee Alphen, GOAL/QPC
   Stephen Barankewicz, Avon Products, Inc.
   Gary Cox, L.A. Darling Company – Wood Division
   John Hussey, Miller Brewing Company
   Robert N. King, RobKingPhotos.com
   Joanna Magazzu, Wyeth Biotech
   Suzan Monastra, Victoria's Secret Production
   Connie Roy-Czyzowski, Northeast Delta Dental
   Robin Snyder, The Griffin Tate Group
   Yvonne Surrey, Y.E.S. Surrey Office Services

How to Use This Book

The Time Management Memory Jogger™ is designed for you to use as a convenient quick reference guide on the job. Put your finger on any improvement tool within seconds! This book uses visual cues, examples, design features, and clear, friendly language to help professionals improve their overall effectiveness.

To Find an Improvement Topic

Use the table of contents at the front of the book, or the icon for that particular improvement method at the beginning of every chapter (samples are shown below).

To Find the Start of Each Improvement Chapter

Look for the blue box at the bottom of the page near the page number.

To Find Special Tips

Look for the areas on checkered backgrounds, with the icon shown.

To Find Additional Information on Included Topics

Look for the sections on pre-hung note cards with blue screened backgrounds. These practical checklists and suggested information provide important cues to better explain the concepts included in the chapter. They will also help you understand the ideas, tools, and techniques you will use to practice better time management.

Notes of Extra Little Tidbits of Useful Information

Look for the pencil and Post-it® Notes for more detailed examples of content from that chapter.

Contents

Introduction

You are about to learn how to spend less time working, while getting more done. That means you will have more free time than you ever thought possible. However, to make this a reality, you will have to work to bring about some changes.

Some of the suggestions in this book involve simple adjustments; others will require more thought and effort up front. Either way, unlike dieting or exercising, the results will be immediate!

Time management involves working on the right things (effectiveness) and doing them the best way (efficiency). This book offers a number of methods you can adopt to help you strike that balance:

- ☺ Track your time to see where it is going. With a clearer picture of how you are spending your time, you can pinpoint the areas that need improvement.

- ☺ Organize everything around you. Disorganization causes you to waste precious time. Once you clear the clutter, you'll be able to think more clearly, make better decisions, and create more effective plans.

- ☺ Set goals and create an action plan. If you don't know where you're going, how will you get there? You have to determine what is most important, set priorities, and then act on your decisions.

- ☺ Work through other time management challenges. Distractions are part of life. Make a plan to avoid time bandits, such as information overload, interruptions, and procrastination.

- ↻ **Examine processes and streamline how you work.** Most of us are creatures of habit. Instead of always doing the work the way you always have, discover a better, faster way.

- ↻ **Reduce time spent in meetings.** Too much time is wasted in unproductive meetings. Pay attention to how your meetings are being conducted and make necessary changes.

- ↻ **Delegate as much as you can.** Do you really have to do everything yourself? Enlist the help of other people so you can spend sufficient time on your core activities.

- ↻ **Discover technology that can save you even more time.** Invest time in learning new technologies that you can use every day. You will finish much faster and make fewer errors. See Improvement Eleven starting on page 155.

To get work done, you actually have to work. Not just be at work, talk about work, or complain about work—but *work*. And to create time for the life you want, you have to work smart.

Time Bandits

The biggest time management mistake people make is not realizing how much time they waste. Work through the following table and see how many opportunities there are for you to make changes. Keep these in mind as you read this book.

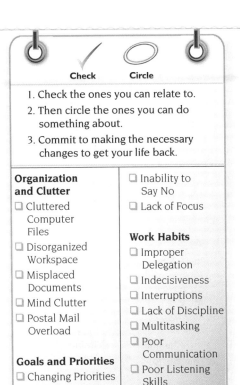

✓ Check   ◯ Circle

1. Check the ones you can relate to.
2. Then circle the ones you can do something about.
3. Commit to making the necessary changes to get your life back.

Organization and Clutter
- ❑ Cluttered Computer Files
- ❑ Disorganized Workspace
- ❑ Misplaced Documents
- ❑ Mind Clutter
- ❑ Postal Mail Overload

Goals and Priorities
- ❑ Changing Priorities
- ❑ Conflicting Priorities
- ❑ Unclear Goals

- ❑ Inability to Say No
- ❑ Lack of Focus

Work Habits
- ❑ Improper Delegation
- ❑ Indecisiveness
- ❑ Interruptions
- ❑ Lack of Discipline
- ❑ Multitasking
- ❑ Poor Communication
- ❑ Poor Listening Skills

Continued...

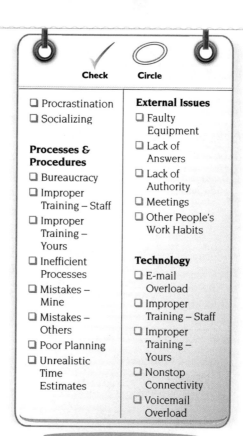

✓ **Check**   ◯ **Circle**

☐ Procrastination	**External Issues**
☐ Socializing	☐ Faulty Equipment
	☐ Lack of Answers
Processes &	☐ Lack of Authority
Procedures	☐ Meetings
☐ Bureaucracy	☐ Other People's Work Habits
☐ Improper Training – Staff	
☐ Improper Training – Yours	**Technology**
☐ Inefficient Processes	☐ E-mail Overload
☐ Mistakes – Mine	☐ Improper Training – Staff
☐ Mistakes – Others	☐ Improper Training – Yours
☐ Poor Planning	☐ Nonstop Connectivity
☐ Unrealistic Time Estimates	☐ Voicemail Overload

You have your work cut out for you. You may even have to give up a couple of weekends to get it all done. But you'll get all that time back and more as you work to simplify and you'll enjoy your life more.

You have to take time to create time. Whatever you want to do more of, *The Time Management Memory Jogger*™ will help you every step of the way.

What Would You Like
to Have More Time to Do?

Improvement One:
Track Where Your Time Goes

Get a clearer picture of how you spend your time.

What is the benefit of tracking my time?

Tracking your time helps you become aware of your actions by visually demonstrating how your time is being spent.

What concepts must I understand to track my time?

You should spend three to four days tracking your time the same way you mind a budget by tracking your spending. If you spend $5 here, $12 there, and $17.50 over there, those expenditures add up. The same thing happens with time.

By tracking your time, you will:

⌁ Realize patterns and trends in your daily work-flow. You may find that you're spending forty-five minutes every morning getting coffee, chatting with co-workers, and reading the paper. What important work could you have finished with that much time to spare?

⊙ **Become better at estimating how long tasks take.** Once you're aware of how long particular tasks actually take, you won't try to cram as many of them into your schedule.

⊙ **Discover how much you multitask.** Rather than focusing on a project that requires undivided blocks of thinking time, you may find yourself jumping from one task to the next without finishing any of them.

What actions must I take to track my time?

Log Your Time

Follow these steps to create a time log and track your activities for a few days.

1. Create a form that captures the information. A scratch pad will do. See page 187 for blank forms.

2. Record the time you spend on all activities, including interruptions.

3. Group similar actions at the end of each day (or tracking period) to determine the percentage of time you spend on each type of activity.

Sample Time Log for Work

Brad's productivity is plummeting. He feels busy and works long hours, but he's not seeing enough positive results. He's decided to keep a time log at work for a few days. He will log each time he has to move from one task to the next. He will also have to list whether activities are planned or interruptions, how important they are, and what other people they involve. The priority scale he has decided to use is A through D, with A being the most important.

Time Log - Work

Time	Activity	Planned	Inter-ruption	Priority (A-D)	People
9:00–10:45	Staff Meeting	Yes. Ran over		B	All Staff
10:48–11:00	Checked e-mail	Yes		C	
11:00–11:12	Phone Call		Yes	A	Client
11:12–11:15	Phone Call		Yes	D	Sales Person
11:15–11:20	Bio Break		Yes	D	Per-sonal
11:20–12:00	Checked e-mail		Yes	C	
12:00–12:35	Surfed, Blogs		Yes	D	
12:35–2:00	Lunch	Yes. Ran over		A	Client
2:00–2:05	Checked e-mail		Yes	C	
2:05–2:10	Phone Call		Yes	C	Joe Brown
2:10–2:12	Visitor		Yes	D	John Smith
2:12–2:30	Checked e-mail			C	

Continued...

Time Log - Work

Time	Activity	Planned	Interruption	Priority (A-D)	People
2:30-3:45	Meeting	Yes. Ran over		C	TS Group
3:45-4:15	Checked e-mail			C	
4:15-4:30	Visitor		Yes	D	Marcy Renn
4:30-4:33	Bio Break		Yes	D	
4:33-5:00	Returned Calls	Yes		B	
5:00-5:22	Looked for files		Yes	D	
5:22-6:30	Core Work	Yes		A	
6:30-7:15	Returned Calls	Yes		B	
7:15-8:00	Checked e-mail	Yes		C	
8:00	Left Work				

Once you understand where your time is going, you'll have a better sense of the adjustments you should make. Following is the list of improvements Brad thinks will help him.

NOTE If your challenges are similar to Brad's, this book can help you learn the necessary skills that will make your life easier, too. Revisit the prioritization scale often as a quick reminder.

Change List

- ❑ Start the day earlier.
- ❑ Organize everything to find things instantly.
- ❑ Prioritize what needs to get done by setting clearer goals.
- ❑ Spend more time on core work.
- ❑ Develop more streamlined processes.
- ❑ Make sure people understand requests.
- ❑ Schedule staff training.
- ❑ Handle interruptions better and learn how to say no.
- ❑ Stop procrastinating.
- ❑ Make meetings more efficient.
- ❑ Delegate as appropriate.
- ❑ Learn software used the most.

Improvement Two:
Start the Day Earlier

Make changes to your daily routine in order to get to work earlier.

What is the benefit of starting my day earlier?

Arriving early to work—before too much activity starts—helps you to concentrate and accomplish important tasks.

What concepts must I understand to start my day earlier?

You will need to have a clear picture of what happens each morning and how long individual tasks take. For example, if you need to get somewhere on time, you have to determine exactly when you

need to leave by counting backward from the time you need to arrive and accounting not only for the time it takes to get there, but also how long it takes to get ready.

What actions must I take to start my day earlier?

⊕ Keep a time log at home for a few days to help you understand where your time is going.

⊕ Determine what changes you can make to your routines to reduce the time spent getting ready.

Time Log for Home

Brad can't figure out why he can never get to work as early as he intends to (at least by 8:00 AM). He's decided to keep a time log for a few mornings.

Time Log - Home

Time	Activity
6:05 am	Alarm went off. Hit the snooze button.
6:10	Alarm went off again. Got out of bed.
6:11–6:32	Stayed in closet putting outfit together.
6:32–6:43	Ironed crease in pants.
6:44–7:20	Downstairs fixing breakfast and lunch, watching the news.
7:21–8:20	Bathroom, including shower and shave.
8:24	Left for work.
8:25–9:00	Commute and made it to the parking garage.
9:00–9:07	Park, got to building.
9:08–9:18	Stopped by cafeteria to buy a coffee.
9:20	At desk.

Continued...

Now that Brad can see in black and white what is happening each morning, he can make a plan to streamline his routine.

New Time Log - Home

NEW - Time	NEW - Activity
6:05 am	Alarm went off. Hit the snooze button.
6:10	Alarm went off again. Got out of bed.
6:11-6:30	Downstairs fixing breakfast. Does not turn on TV. Had prepared clothes and lunch the night before. Also fixed Thermos® of coffee (from the automatic coffee maker, also set the night before).
6:31-7:30	Bathroom, including shower and shave.
7:31	Left for work.
7:31-8:30	Commute and made it into the parking garage. Trip was longer because traffic is worse that early in the morning.
8:30-8:37	Park, got to building.
8:39	At desk. (No more stopping by the cafeteria.)

Still not in at 8 am.

The Time Management Memory Jogger™ | ©2008 GOAL/QPC

Brad is still not getting to work as early as he wants to. After counting backward from the time he wants to arrive at his office, and considering how long it takes him to get ready, it's obvious that Brad needs to get up earlier each morning to be in by 8 am.

Get Out of the House on Time

When you leave home late, your day has barely started and already you're stressed out. You might even have to finish putting on makeup or shaving while driving. Perhaps you will have to make that same phone call to apologize for being late. You secretly promise yourself that tomorrow will start out better, but without making some changes to ensure that outcome, that promise is merely a good intention.

Simple planning will make life easier, and that includes getting out of the house on time. Fortunately there are several steps you can take right now to make sure that happens.

Things to Do This Weekend

① Purge and organize your closet, remembering that if you didn't wear it last year, you probably won't wear it this year. Separate the things you want to keep from those that can go, bag items to give away or consign, and dump the rest. Arrange your closet by styles (casual vs. business), keeping like things together (all your pants/skirts, jackets, blouses/shirts should be grouped together), sorting by color. If you never mix and match, hang complete outfits together and keep them in the jacket section by color, light to dark.

⊕ Iron next week's clothes or set up a routine to do it during the week. (Spray starch makes ironing easier.)

⊕ Hang clocks all over the house, especially near the bathroom and dressing areas. You'll be able to pace yourself better because you'll have a clear sense of time.

⊕ De-junk the garage so you can park your car in it. That way you won't have to spend time warming the car or de-icing windows.

⊕ Run errands that include: getting several sets of your keys made, having your hair cut into a quick and easy-to-keep style, and gassing up your car for the week (if you ride public transportation every day, buy a monthly pass). Keep change in your car for tolls or purchase a "cruise card" so you will not have to stop at all.

Batch similar activities in a logical order. For example, wait until next week to buy a new headset because your dental appointment is near the computer store.

Or perhaps you need to go to the bank, post office, and dry cleaners. Which one closes first and which errand is the most important? Map your trip based on these factors.

*Here is a sample errand pad you
could use while you are out.*

Date (or week of):	Objective this week:	
TO DO WHILE I'M OUT (prioritize with ABCD)	**TO CONTACT WHILE I'M OUT** (call or e-mail)	**STATUS** (done, busy, left msg., etc.)
Task priority - ABCD		
TO BUY - Office: supplies, etc.	**TO BUY** - Home: groceries, etc	
NOTES:		

Things to Do the Night Before

⊕ Set the breakfast table after dinner and set out the cereal box, too. Put the milk in a container that smaller kids can handle and place things they want often on lower shelves. Fill your coffee pot and set the timer for the morning.

⊕ Make the lunches (right after dinner is the best time). Put an empty grocery bag by the door that you leave by as a reminder to bring your lunch (grocery bag=food=get lunch).

⊕ Check your calendar and prepare everything you'll need for the next day. Pack the car with the things you'll need to take with you (or put everything near the door that you leave by).

⊕ Choose outfits and accessories (or at least have a good idea of what you will wear the next day). Keep your wardrobe and jewelry very simple, especially when you're traveling.

Things to Do That Morning

⊕ Be the first to arise early enough in the morning so you can have quiet time alone. Get others up based on how long it takes them to get ready. For example, if you have to comb your daughter's hair, it's going to take you longer to get her ready than your son, so she should get up first.

⊕ Use a kitchen timer to time everything you do so you can create a morning schedule that works for you. Don't watch TV unless you build extra time into your routine for the distraction.

⊙ Carry the same pocketbook and briefcase every day and make sure they have many compartments. Always keep items in the same place, especially your keys.

⊙ Determine how long it takes you to reach your destination. Time yourself from the moment you leave to the time you are inside where you need to be. Adjust your morning schedule accordingly.

NOTE You can't change how much time you get every day, but you can get more out of the time you have by changing your habits.

Improvement Three:
Get Organized

Eliminate clutter everywhere and create a system for finding anything fast.

What is the benefit of getting organized?

Creating a customized system helps you save time because you'll be able to find what you need when you need it.

What concepts must I understand to get organized?

Disorganization can cost you hours of wasted time. You should apply the same organizing principles to everything from your clothes closet to your computer files. Once you arrange everything logically, you (and others) will be able to find what you need right away.

TIP Principles of Organizing

The principles of organizing can be applied to any project or situation, whether it is for your clothes closet, garage, or office.

- Purge on a regular basis, and keep only things you value, love, or need.

- Keep like items together (*e.g., all writing instruments, all shipping supplies, etc.*)

- Give everything a home and keep it there when you are not using it.

- Put everything near its point of use and make it convenient to get to it, even if you have to buy duplicates (*e.g., scissors and tape on the desk and on the work table*).

- Use the right product to store your item even if it is intended to be used for something else (*e.g., clear shower caps to store cut melons in the refrigerator*).

The following excuses could block your progress.

Excuse 1: I Don't Have Time
Disorganized people don't have any time to do most things they want to do *because* they are disorganized. A moderately disorganized person loses as many as 240 hours a year (based on a 40-hour week) looking for things at work.

Excuse 2: I Don't Know How
It's possible no one ever taught you how to get organized. Some people have a natural propensity toward organization and others have to work very hard at it. The good news is that anyone can learn this skill.

Excuse 3: I Know Where Everything Is
You do know where *some* things are, but mainly because you've dug through those piles so many times you have memorized them. This is not a system. If something happens to you, could anyone else be able to find anything in your office? Could anyone else run your business or manage your project?

Continued...

Plus:
- It takes too long to get to it when it's in a pile.
- It's impossible to gather related work quickly.
- It's a waste of brain cells to memorize piles.

Excuse 4: It's Nobody Else's Business
Unless you own the business, it certainly is someone else's business that disorganization is affecting your productivity. And if you own the business, realize that everything you do has a domino effect. If your business is mired in chaos how can you be successful?

Excuse 5: I Got Organized Once but the Clutter Came Back
In order to keep the piles from coming back, you have to set up systems for handling everything and then maintain them vigilantly.

Excuse 6: I Want to Look Busy
Being disorganized does not mean you are busy: it means you are not working up to your full potential because you are wasting too much time. Moreover, you are impeding someone else's progress. *Continued...*

EXCUSE 7: I'm a Creative Type and Can't Get Organized

A lot of research has been done in recent years that explains the concept of right- and left-brain dominance. Creative people, whether they are artists, homemakers, or executives, often have particular problems with organization because, as scientific studies have shown, creativity resides in the right hemisphere of the brain. The left hemisphere is where the concept of time, structure, detail, and analytic ability reside. But even right-brain thinkers can get organized if they design a system that fits their style.

What actions must I take to get organized?

Most people have to learn how to get organized. It's best to start with a plan.

- Block out some time on your calendar to make it happen.
- Learn the basic principles and follow through on them.
- Create a system for everything you need to keep.
- Maintain that system every day.

You will have to make very brutal decisions about every piece of paper in those piles on the desk, on the floor, behind the door, in the cabinets, and every other place they've accumulated. Separate your keepers from your discards, and recycle, trash, or shred as you go.

With trash bags as your closest ally, choose an area and start!

TIP *In deciding what to keep and what to throw out, ask yourself*:

When was the last time I referred to this?
Eighty percent of those papers you insist on keeping will never be referred to again. PURGE!

Do I need to keep it for legal or personal reasons?
Your attorney, accountant, records management department, or your secretary of state's office can help you determine how long to keep files (legally). On the other hand, even if it is something you love or value, you will have to purge enough other items to make room for it. PURGE!

Can I get the information somewhere else?
Just about anything you need to know is on the Internet; years worth of bank statements are filed at the bank; utility

Continued...

TIP

companies have electronic copies of your
bills; the creator of the document has it
on file; and so on. PURGE!

**If I throw it out and need it later, can
I live with the consequences of having
thrown it out?**
In most cases, of course you can,
especially if you didn't create it. Unless
you are the company librarian, you
cannot justify keeping years worth of
what amounts to junk. PURGE!

NOTE: Just because someone sent you something or gave you something doesn't mean you have to keep it.

Know How Long to Keep Files

Your records management department, tax attorney, accountant, the Internal Revenue Service, or your secretary of state's office can help you determine how long you have to keep certain files. The following will give you an idea of how long you could keep your personal and business files. This list is provided by Blythe, White & Associates, CPA, Paducah, Kentucky, and is to only be used as a general guideline.

How Long to Keep Information

Individual

Bank Deposit Slips	3 Years
Bank Statements	6 Years
Cancelled Checks	3 Years
Divorce Decrees and Dependent Agreements	3 Years
Expense Reports	3 Years
Investment Account Statements	
Nonretirement	3 Years After the Sale
Retirement	3 Years After the Sale, Rollover, or Distribution
Real Estate Records	Permanently
Tax Returns	Permanently
Supporting Documents for Tax Returns	7 Years

Continued...

How Long to Keep Information cont.

Business

Accident Reports/Claims (Settled Cases)	7 Years
Accounts Payable Ledgers and Schedules	7 Years
Accounts Receivable Ledgers and Schedules	8 Years
Audit Reports	Permanently
Bank Statements	3 Years
Capital Stock and Bond Records: Ledgers, Transfer Registers, Stubs Showing Issues, Record of Interest Coupons, Options, etc.	Permanently
Charts of Accounts	Permanently
Checks (Cancelled Checks for Important Payments, Special Contracts, Purchase of Assets, Payment of Taxes, etc.) Checks Should Be Filed With the Papers Pertaining to the Underlying Transaction	Permanently

Continued...

How Long to Keep Information cont.

Checks (Cancelled Except Those Noted Before)	7 Years
Contracts and Leases (Expired)	7 Years
Contracts and Leases Still Active	Permanently
Correspondence, General and Schedules	2 Years
Correspondence, Legal and Important Letters	Permanently
Correspondence, Routine With Customers/Vendors	2 Years
Deeds, Mortgages and Bills of Sale	Permanently
Depreciation Schedules	Permanently
Employee Personnel Records (After Termination)	7 Years
Employment Applications	3 Years
Financial Statements (Year-end, Other Months Optional)	Permanently
General Ledgers, Year-end Trial Balances	Permanently
Insurance Records, Policies, etc.	Permanently

Continued...

How Long to Keep Information cont.

Internal Audit Reports (Miscellaneous)	3 Years
Inventory Records	7 Years
Invoices to Customers or from Vendors	7 Years
IRA and Keogh Plan Contributions, Rollovers, Transfers and Distribution	Permanently
Minutes Books of Directors, Stockholders, Bylaws & Charters	Permanently
Payroll Records, Summaries, and Tax Returns	7 Years
Petty Cash Vouchers	3 Years
Property Records, Including Costs, Depreciation Reserves, Year-end Trial Balances, Depreciation Schedules, Blueprints, and Plans	Permanently
Purchase Orders	3 Years
Receiving Sheets	1 Year
Safety Records	6 Years

Continued...

How Long to Keep Information cont.

Sales Records	7 Years
Stock and Bond Certificates (Cancelled)	7 Years
Subsidiary Ledgers	7 Years
Tax Returns, Revenue Agents' Reports, and Other Documents Relating to Determination of Income Tax Liability	Permanently
Time Cards and Daily Reports	7 Years
Trademark Registrations, Patents, and Copyrights	Permanently
Voucher Register and Schedules	7 Years
Vouchers for Payments to Vendors, Employees, etc. (Includes Allowances and Reimbursements of Employees, Officers, etc., for Travel and Entertainment Expenses)	7 Years

Gather the Right Supplies

Before you get started, gather the following supplies so you won't have to get up while you are working.

Supplies You Will Need	Why You Need Them
Large trash bags and a shredder	Most of the clutter you will go through can be trashed. Do not stop to shred —you can do this later.
Envelopes and mailers, shipping labels, stamps, a postal scale or meter, access to business and company directories (online and paper), and an Outbox	You will find items that need to be mailed or returned. Package them completely and put them in the Outbox before moving to the next item.
Clear plastic folders labeled: TO DO, TO FILE, TO FAX, TO COPY, TO READ, TO RESPOND, and PENDING	You should batch all similar work. Later, you can make one trip to the copier, fax everything at once, and write all letters and send all e-mails while you are in a writing mode.

Continued...

Supplies You Will Need	Why You Need Them
Fax cover sheets	Complete this at your desk and keep everything you need to fax together in your TO FAX folder.
Your calendar	You might need to schedule meetings and other events that you had forgotten about.
Tickler (follow-up) file or notebook (with slots for each of a month's 1–31 days)	When you have paper that goes with a task or meeting, file it in the appropriate due date.
Spiral notebook (your to-do book)	Jot down miscellaneous tasks you will need to complete. Some items will go in the book, some in Outlook Tasks, some on an errand pad, etc.

Eliminate Piles One at a Time

Eliminate clutter one pile at a time. Sort the papers into separate piles (or folders), trashing, shredding, or recycling as you go. Use "keep" categories such as: TO DO, TO FILE, TO FAX, TO COPY, TO READ, TO RESPOND, TO MAIL, TO RETURN, and PENDING, so that things you are keeping won't have to be separated again. Set up a special place for papers that need to be recycled or shredded (you can even pay your children to do this later).

Do Something With Everything You Touch

Starting with one pile at a time, pick up each piece of paper and make a quick decision about it. Here are some things you might come across and suggestions on how to handle them.

NOTE   If you stand while going through your piles, you will make quicker decisions.

What You Will Find	What to Do With It
Notice of a meeting you have to attend.	You have your calendar right there so schedule it. If you need to keep the notice, put it in your tickler file for the day of the meeting. Your tickler file is labeled with the dates Jan–Dec 1–31.
Small project you need to work on that is due next month.	Schedule time on your calendar to work on it, highlight the due date, and put it in your tickler file for the day you have scheduled to work on it.
Handful of small project work.	If the work is important and you can finish it in 2–3 minutes, go ahead and do it.

Continued… |

What You Will Find	What to Do With It
Document you need to file.	If you need to keep it, put it in the To File pile. (Once you create a better filing system, you will always file it right away.)
Several reports and books borrowed from people.	Package them, affix postage, and put them in your Outbox.
Work you should do this week.	Batch similar work in the appropriate folder (e.g., TO COPY, TO RESPOND).
Several documents all related to one project.	Keep all related project work together. Use clear, plastic folders or regular file folders for simple projects. A binder might work for more complex projects.

Continued...

What You Will Find	What to Do With It
Report you need to finish but you are waiting for a co-worker to finalize his part.	This particular project is low priority, so put it in your PENDING file (because you are waiting on someone else to do something). Track the project's due date in whatever system you have set up.
Information you receive that you never read.	Send an e-mail asking to be taken off the distribution list.
Letter you need to send a quick response to.	Write a legible note on the letter and send it back. Alternatively, e-mail the response.
Letter you need to respond to but you need time to think about it.	Put this in your TO RESPOND folder and write all letters later in one sitting.

Continued...

What You Will Find	What to Do With It
Magazines you never read.	Send label to publishers to cancel the subscriptions.
Stacks of business cards.	Trash most of these. For the few that you will keep, scan them or type into a database.
Magazines and newspapers with articles you want to keep.	Tear out the articles you want to keep and set up a file for them, separating them by category so it will be easy to retrieve later. Then throw the magazines out. Keep some articles in your purse or briefcase so you can read while waiting for appointments, etc.
Bills you need to pay.	Open bills as they come in, time stamp them if you need to, *Continued...*

What You Will Find	What to Do With It
	and trash the ads stuffed inside. Then find a convenient place to put them and create a routine for handling them once or twice a month. Once the bills are paid, keep the receipt portions together until you get that month's bank statement. Staple all of these together and keep them with any pay stubs you receive that month.
Information you want to discuss at the next staff meeting.	Keep them in a Meetings folder for each type you attend.
Documents that should go to staff.	Add a routing slip to each and indicate how *Continued...*

What You Will Find	What to Do With It
	they should be handled or directed. Put it in your Outbox.
Bits of paper with miscellaneous information.	Put everything in a logical place: a Word document, affix to a page in your to-do book, add to your database, etc.
Work you need to delegate.	Develop a way to track the work before you forward it. If it is something that requires a lot of detailed instruction, schedule a face-to-face meeting with the employee.
Complex work you need to work on.	Schedule uninterrupted time to plan and schedule the project.

Getting rid of clutter is exhausting but you can do it. This exercise will help you keep up with your workload instead of being blindsided by forgotten appointments or deadlines. It can be exhausting but you can do it. Take breaks if you need to and be proud of your efforts.

> NOTE
>
> If your eyes always see a mess, your mind will become one.

Create a Place for Everything

It is time to revisit all those items you decided to keep and make some decisions about what to do with them. To make this process bearable, you will have to establish a set place for everything and keep everything in its place.

In other words:

- ☺ Create a logical filing system and maintain it daily.
- ☺ Set up your workspace with the right layout and supplies.

Create a Filing System That Works

A filing system should be logical so there is never any doubt about where you have filed something. Moreover, anyone else needing something in your files should be able to find it.

You probably wouldn't shop at a bookstore where the books were just piled on the shelves in no particular order. What you'd want to find would be shelves organized based on the broadest category first, which is genre (the sci-fi books in one place, literature in another, biographies somewhere else, and so on). The subcategory of each genre would be alphabetical by author name. This is the same logic you will use to organize anything.

To create a logical filing system, break down your job duties or business functions as if in an outline. Use nouns to create broad categories that include: Accounting, Administrative, Human Resources, Legal, Marketing, and Reference. Then add more broad categories specific to what you do, such as Sales if you are a sales professional, Issues if you are a magazine editor, and so on. Once you establish your broad categories, create a logical breakdown for each one.

 Use this same system for your computer files and your e-mail Inbox.

A subject-based filing system like this will help you when it is time to archive files (because you will already have like media types filed together.) Use the A to Z system only for vendor- or client-only files or something similar.

To create a logical filing system, follow these steps:

1. Create a filing index for all the files you will keep. You'll refer to this when you forget where

you filed something, and you'll know approximately how many file folders to buy.

2. Use hanging and interior file folders to help keep everything separated. Use a unique colored tab to distinguish the main categories.

3. Type your labels or use a label maker. If you make your system neat and attractive, you'll take more pride in it and will better maintain it.

4. Arrange your hanging folders so they face you when you open the drawer. Put all your plastic

tabs in a straight line, one behind the other, putting them in the front of the folder instead of the back. Tabs in a straight line are easier on the eyes, and you won't have to worry about changing tab positions when you add more later.

5. Stagger the folders inside the hanging folders when you have more than one subcategory.

6. Maintain the system every day and purge it yearly.

Complete Filing Index

A filing index is an outline—a logical organization that is customized to fit your needs. Eventually you will know your system so well you won't need to refer to the index, but others will. For every piece of paper, assign it to the broadest category first (based on how the item will be retrieved), then determine the subcategory.

The next few pages will detail the best way to set up your file folder structure. Refer back to this each year to update things that you may not have used this year.

While a document is still in your hand, file it—don't pile it! Taking two seconds to put a document back into the file will save you minutes, and sometimes hours, the next time you go looking for it. If you don't need it, trash or shred it NOW!

TIP File it Based on Retrieval

Reggie is a recruiter. He has collected many resumes at career fairs, which have piled up everywhere you can imagine. He was having little luck interviewing potential candidates because he couldn't find their information. By the time he would find their resumes, they had already found employment elsewhere.

All he needs is a logical filing system. The resumes he collected were from all over the country, and they fit into four job types. They need to be filed based on how he would retrieve them. In this case, first by region (because his boss wants to know what is happening geographically) then by job type.

Referring to instructions on how to create a logical filing system, the broadest category for Reggie is "Recruitment" (a broad category that is specific for his job). "Resumes" would be an appropriate subcategory. Under "Resumes" the first breakdown would be "Region" and within each region, the resumes would be separated by job type (if he were not a recruiter, "Recruitment" would be a subcategory of "Human Resources").

Suggested Structure for File System:

Directories
File Index (Keep your File Index in the front of your files.)
Add various company directories that you refer to often to this hanging folder.

Work Folders (You may prefer to keep these in a desktop file instead of a drawer.)
>   HOT
>   Follow Up (Your tickler file)
>   Pending (You are waiting on someone else to
>   do something before you can finish.)
>>   Meetings
>>   Projects
>>   Prospects
>>   Other

Mail
Create mail folders if you are a support person. This is mail for the boss. Use various colors for each category of mail (Action, Read, Signature, etc.).

Projects
>   Current Projects
>>   *Create a separate plastic or manila folder for
>>   each project.*
>   Pending Projects
>>   *Create a separate plastic or manila folder for
>>   each project.*

Continued...

Accounting

Bills to Pay
  Bills Paid (File here once paid or in Receipts file below)
Accounts Receivable (A/R: People who owe you. You will not need this if you use accounting software.)
  A/R (Current Year)
  A/R Closed
Audit
Banking
  Bank Statements (Current Year)
  Deposit Slips (Current Year)
Receipts (Current Year) – Another option for filing receipts is to keep them with the bank statement for the month during which the money was spent.
  AMEX
  VISA
  Other
Tax Info
  CPA
  General Info

Administrative

E-mail/Internet/Intranet
  E-mail
  Internet/Intranet
Equipment
  Computers
  Copier
  Fax
  Other Equipment
  Printers

History
Historical Events
Photos
How Things Work (Instructions on various tools, etc.)
Insurance
(Business-related, not health)
Shipping
Air Overnight (Labels, etc.)
UPS™ or FedEx®
USPS®
Security
Pass Codes, etc.
Supply Orders

Business (Rename this category to fit your needs. Customize this entire category based on your job or business.)
Budget (If you did not need Accounting category above)
Clients (Create A–Z tabs if you have lots so you can keep them sorted.)
Goals & Objectives

Human Resources
Accolades (Yours)
Awards/Recognition Programs
Benefits (Health, Vision, etc.)
Education/Training
Certificates
Classes/Seminars/Workshops
Future Training Ideas

Continued...

Employee Personnel Files (Create a folder for each person. Keep these files in locked drawer.)
Resumes/Bios (Separate based on how you will retrieve them: geographic area, job type)

Legal
Agreements & Contracts
Incorporation Papers
Proposals

Marketing
Advertisements (your business)
Collateral
Brochures
Sales Kits
Competition
Database
Database Input (Keep business cards here until you put them in a database.)
Future Ideas/Samples
Networking (Add all groups you belong to/network with.)
Newsletter (company newsletters)
Public Relations
Articles (about you or your company)
Blog/Zine
Campaigns
Media Kit
Print
Radio
TV
Web

Continued...

Research Info
Demographics
Focus Groups
Surveys
Seminars (If you give them to promote your business.)
Web site (If you have one.)
Host (Hosting company, contact phone numbers, etc.)
Future Ideas for Site
Scheduled Updates
Visitor Comments
Site Changes

Meetings (If you do not attend many meetings, add Meetings to Administrative category)
Board Meetings
Agenda/Minutes – Board Meetings
Future Board Meetings (items want to cover in next meeting)
Department Meetings
Agenda/Minutes – Department Meetings
Future Meetings (items you want to cover in next meeting)
Division Meetings
Agenda/Minutes– Division Meetings
Future Meetings (items you want to cover in next meeting)
Employee Meetings (Create hanging and interior folders for each appropriate employee.)
Retreats – Staff, Company
Travel Information (General) (Or put this info under Administrative.)
Car Rentals

Continued...

> *Expense Statements*
> *Frequent Flyer*
> *Hotels*
> *Maps/Directions*
> *Travel Archives (Use this section to keep*
> *all travel documentation by client in*
> *alphabetical order.)*

Forms
Create a special section in a file drawer if you have
paper forms.

Reference This file holds large reference material.
Group like subjects together.

> Articles/News clippings (Break down by
> categories appropriate to your own work)
> > *Computer – Articles*
> > *Entertainment – Articles*
> > *Human Resources – Articles*
> > > *Diversity – Articles*
> > > *EEO – Articles*
> > > *Harassment – Articles*
> > *Sports – Articles*
> > *Vacation Spots – Articles*
> Presentations (Background material)
> > *Humorous*
> > *Quotes*
> > *Statistics*
> > *Trends*

Vendors
This could be catalogs from vendors, consultant
info, and so on. Group like subjects together, then
by alphabetical order.

Set Up Your Workspace

Now that the piles are gone and you can see your furniture, create a special place for everything so you can find it the instant you need it. Write down everything that is already working for you. Then write how you wish everything could be. For example, if you know you enjoy looking out the window as you work, but a huge filing cabinet blocks your view, you know you will have to design a layout that will fix this.

Put items you use most often closest to you and arrange your office so that you don't have to get up to do things that you do often.

Move Desktop Gadgets and Gizmos

All those electronic gadgets and gizmos you have add to desktop clutter. In addition to using a flat screen monitor, here are two additional ways to free up more space:

- ① Attach a piece of pegboard under your desk and use wiring or strong tape to attach all your gadgets to it, including the outlet strip for ideas on how to do this, visit www.decluttered.com.

- ① Place a small table next to or behind your desk and move the gadgets there.

The Junk Drawer

The best way to tackle a junk drawer is to dump the contents out onto your desk. Go through everything and throw out as you go, including all those condiment packs you have collected over the years, pens that don't write, crumpled paper napkins, and the many doodads you have collected over the years. Use a drawer organizer with compartments and slots to create a home for everything.

Always measure your space and drawers before you buy new ones.

Credenza Clutter

The credenza is usually packed full of useless papers, books, office supplies you didn't know you had, trinkets from meetings and events from long, long ago, and a host of other items that can be thrown out at a second glance.

Starting with one drawer at a time, use the same process you have learned for tackling clutter (purge and sort). If you have items in your credenza that are taking up precious file space, get rid of them or find somewhere else to put them. Use these drawers to store reference material and other files that you need to keep.

NOTE — File drawers are too precious to use for anything but files.

Bookshelf Clutter

The office bookshelf is commonly used to store old notebooks full of outdated material, books from classes for software you no longer use, and books you would like to keep for reference.

You can easily improve the functionality of your office bookshelf. Once you eliminate the excess, use these tips to improve its order and appearance.

- ① Create binder spine inserts so you know at a glance each notebook's contents.

- ① Arrange books according to topic (e.g., Management, Marketing, Personal Improvement). To make reshelving simple, you could establish a color scheme using transparent stickers and assign a color to each topic. It will be easier to put your management book back in the right place because you'll put it where the other red stickers are, for example.

NOTE Add a special color sticker to denote books you have already read so you can skip them when looking for something new.

- ① Purchase bookends so the books will stand straight and look neater.

- ① Put some type of greenery on the top shelf, or on one of the other shelves, to make your bookshelf more attractive. The more attractive it is, the more likely you are to maintain its appearance.

For any other items you have on your bookshelf, apply the organizing principles of putting like things together. In addition, get into the habit of putting things back when you have finished with them.

Organize Computer Files

If you do not organize your computer files logically, you could spend hours trying to find a document. When you save your files, remember these important points:

- ⊕ Use the same concept for creating your computer filing system as you did with your paper filing system (separate into broad categories, then break them down into subcategories). You should duplicate the system although you will probably have more computer than paper files.

- ⊕ Give your files sensible names that will make it easy to find the one you need.

- ⊕ Establish a file naming convention to easily identify which team member created the document, when it was created, and what it is about. For example, "020108jt_tips on getting out of the house on time.doc" is a document that was typed on February 1, 2008, by someone with the initials "jt." The filename is sensible enough so you will know exactly what the document is about.

  You could also place the filename in the footer of your document. For example, in Microsoft Word, use an AutoText entry to insert the filename and path into the document. (See graphic on next page.)

Every document you create in Microsoft® Word is based on a template. The default template is called "normal.dot." If you add this AutoText entry to the footer of this template, the filename will automatically appear on every document that is based on it. Refer to Word's Help for more information. Other word processing programs should have similar options.

You may be thinking that none of this is necessary because you can use Google™ Desktop Search (or the lesser known Copernic® and MSN® Desktop Search) to find the files you need. First, some companies block the use of this technology. Second, why would you want to explore a long list of search results, trying to figure out which document you need? Third, you will have an impossible time of sending files to archives if like items are not saved together. If you follow the system explained herein, you will be able to find the files you need without wasting time.

Organize Your Schedule

Overscheduling commitments is another form of clutter. Continuing to cram too much into your work-day will diminish the benefits gained from getting organized, such as having more time to think and plan. Good calendar management can be achieved by following some simple rules.

How to Schedule Work

⊙ Declare "No Meeting" days. Set aside certain days of the week so you can get important work done. Mark these as busy days on your calendar and then stick to it.

   After a vacation, tell your staff or co-workers you will be back in the office on Wednesday, but come in on Monday. You'll have two meeting-free days to catch up.

⊙ Schedule anything that you are required to attend. Board meetings, your daughter's soccer game, a PTA meeting, or a neighborhood gathering—record them all. And don't commit to anything unless you are looking at your calendar.

⊙ Add contact information. Note the phone numbers of all people you schedule meetings with; the number will come in handy if you get lost or run into traffic.

⊙ Leave time between meetings to catch up. Use the time between meetings to handle any action items that can be done quickly.

- ⊕ **Allow for travel time.** You need enough time to get to and from your destination, so block this time off on your calendar. Be realistic about this time and account for the extra minutes it will take you to find a parking space, get from your car to the building, and sign in with security and/or reception.

- ⊕ **Conduct pre-call planning.** If you have a standard list of essential questions, create a checklist. This will help you stay on point during the meeting.

- ⊕ **Confirm appointments.** Confirming appointments is not always necessary, but each situation is different. For example, corporate executives generally don't need to confirm appointments with other corporate executives. However, if you are a salesperson meeting with a busy potential customer, send a confirming e-mail message the day before or call the day of.

- ⊕ **Respect the person you are meeting with.** Hold all calls, ignore all beeps, and resist working on nonrelated items during the meeting.

- ⊕ **Know the next step.** You will have to do some type of follow-on work after an appointment—make sure you know what it is.

When to Schedule Work

⊕ Get to work before the action starts. If activity is nonstop, perhaps you can work at home in the morning to get important tasks done and then go to the office.

⊕ Do work you dread first and get it over with (if it is important). Once you finish work you don't look forward to, you can enjoy the rest of your day. Get creative and develop a simpler way to do it or delegate it. Technology might be a solution.

⊕ Schedule blocks of time for complex projects. Knowledge work requires focus in discrete intervals. You will do a better quality job if you schedule your thinking time.

⊕ Follow your biological schedule if you can. If you're not a morning person, schedule routine tasks that don't require much effort for the morning hours. Save the complex work for later.

⊕ Become a morning person if you have to. If you have no choice about when you need to get going in the morning, don't wear yourself out at night. Turn off the television and go to bed. Develop a morning routine that will boost your energy level.

⊕ Close out the day by getting ready for tomorrow. You will feel in control if you wake up knowing what you need to do, where you are going, and how to get there.

Organize for the Road

Getting and staying organized takes extra planning if you're a road warrior.

ⓘ Create a travel file. Keep everything you will need for your trip in one place, including meeting papers, ticket, itinerary, etc.

ⓘ Minimize gadgets. Take only what you need and purchase mini versions of whatever you can. For example, a mini USB hub comes in handy if your laptop doesn't have enough ports. Another helpful tool is Outlets To Go, a mini power strip that folds into itself and fits anywhere.

ⓘ Expense report receipts. Create a system to organize your receipts while you're traveling, which makes it easier to submit reports later.

　ⓘ Organize. Keep a letter-sized envelope marked "Receipts CityName/EventName" in your wallet or laptop bag (because you will always have this with you).

　ⓘ Collect and store. File receipts immediately. If you are in a taxi or limo, get the driver to fill one out (at minimum, the date and amount).

⊕ **Complete report.** Be diligent about completing your expense report, working on it during your spare moments (in your hotel room, on the plane, etc.).

For an electronic solution for managing receipts, NEATReceipts™ is a small scanner that is light enough for travel. You can scan into PDF format, analyze, and organize your receipts, bills, and business cards, then store everything in a database on your computer.

An Organized Vehicle

If your vehicle is your office, now is a good time to get it organized. Your local office supply or auto parts store has organizing products to use in setting up a mini office in your car, whether you use your front seat, back seat, or the trunk.

You can use a milk crate to hold hanging files for company forms you use often, such as fax cover sheets, sales forms, or marketing brochures. Create other sections for items such as scissors, tape, pre-stamped note cards, letterhead and envelopes, letter opener, postage stamps in several denominations, extra money for the tollbooth, calculator, screwdriver, measuring tape, and other items you have needed in the past.

Packing Tips

You should pack according to how many activities you will attend and take as little as possible, using the agenda as your guide.

TIP Packing Tips

❑ **Make copies of important documents.** Take copies of your major credit cards, passport, driver's license, insurance card, etc., with you. Arrange them on the copier platen in such a way as to keep the number of copies to a minimum.

❑ **Use a clothing color scheme.** Stick to two colors and wear outfits that can be interchanged and worn with the same pair of shoes.

❑ **Keep like items together.** Use plastic bags to keep complete outfits together. Keep all facial products in a small plastic bag, all nail products in another, and so on. Replenish everything after your trip (to find a great assortment of travel-size products, visit *www.minimus.biz*).

❑ **Prioritize by order of use.** Put the first thing you will need upon arrival on the top and pack your most wrinkle-resistant clothing on the bottom (unless you need it first).

Continued...

TIP *Packing Tips*

- ☐ **Keep shoes separate from clothes.** Use a plastic or fabric bag to store shoes.

- ☐ **Tuck some things inside others.** Put small items inside bigger ones. Roll your socks and belts and place them in leftover corners and spaces.

- ☐ **Keep accessories to a minimum.** Use the same earrings and necklace, ring, and watch – every day. Use a reversible belt that will match anything you wear.

- ☐ **Include an empty, rugged bag that folds and zips.** If you get to the airport and find your bag is too heavy, you will be able to fill this one and check it. For easy access, keep it in an outside compartment of your luggage.

Other Peoples' Messes

The inefficient work habits of the people around you can cause your productivity to plummet. You can't plan effectively if you're working amid chaos, without written processes, or a clear mission from your leadership team. You will spend your day putting out fires, backtracking, starting over, and not getting anywhere.

A Messy Boss

No one will affect your time at work more than your immediate manager. If your boss doesn't run a tight ship, don't you feel the leaks? How many times have you had to drop everything you were doing to deal with an emergency caused by someone else's disorganization: a report that was due yesterday but has been buried in a pile, a project that was poorly defined resulting in a workproduct that had to be redone, a frenzied ride to a meeting across town to drop off crucial materials someone forgot?

There is a difference between fast-paced and total chaos. If you are the boss, everything you do filters down to everyone else. Lead by example and invest the necessary time to get your act together. Are you the reason Mary rarely gets to see Little Johnny play ball? If you are, shame on you.

What to Do About It: Find the Pain

A disorganized person—in this case your boss—is experiencing some type of problem that would resolve itself with the implementation of better work habits. If you can help your boss figure out what he's missing out on, you can also offer him suggestions or simple solutions that can help.

TIP It's Time for a Meeting

Schedule time with your boss to discuss how getting organized would benefit him or her (*not* how it will benefit you). Do some research before the meeting and review your boss's job description, performance plan, or sales plan (or whatever you can find) so that you will understand what criteria he is being measured against.

Identify the pain that is a byproduct of the chaos (such as missing deadlines on projects, etc.), and show him how simple solutions can make that pain go away.

A Messy Co-worker

Messy co-workers can wreak havoc in your day, especially if what they do has anything to do with what you do. You could try the same technique of suggesting solutions to the obvious problems that are causing their disorganization. If this doesn't work, you should get management involved.

But if you find that management just wants the work done, regardless of the extra hours you have to put in, it might be time to check your goals and values, to augment your job skills on your own time, and to start planning your next move.

Improvement Four:
Set Goals and Priorities

Determine what you want to achieve and put a plan in place to do it.

What is the benefit of setting goals and priorities?

Prioritizing activities based on their value helps you focus on what is most important.

What concepts must I understand to set goals and priorities?

You have to establish a vision, set goals, list objectives, and create an action plan to get to where you want to go. You can't just dream it. Your ultimate destination is your vision. To make your vision a reality, you have to set goals. Your objectives are the details that will help you achieve your goals. Finally, your action plan outlines the work you have to do to reach each objective.

What actions must I take to set goals and priorities?

To achieve your goals, you will have to do more than just scribble a wish list or talk about what you want to accomplish. You will have to make a concerted effort in a specific direction.

Vision

Your vision should represent your ultimate destination. Perhaps you can see yourself in a chair in front of your fabulous beach house where you are enjoying a very early retirement.

Goal

To make your vision possible, you will set a goal to, say, increase the number of sales you close so you can make more money so you can afford the beach house.

Objectives

Your objectives help you reach a goal. They must:

⊕ Be specific.

⊕ Have a deadline.

⊕ Be measurable.

⊕ Be attainable (but not too easy).

One of your objectives could be to learn how to play golf so you can network more with key decision makers on the golf course. Consequently, one of your objectives would read like this:

Not this: I will learn how to play golf.

But this: I will begin golf lessons in September of this year, and will be able to at least hit the ball by December.

Action Plan

Your action plan is a detailed outline of everything you need to do to accomplish each objective. In our example, it would look something like this:

1. Notify my neighborhood association that I will not be able to serve on the board this year (so that you will have more free time).

2. Call around to find golf clinics near my house and schedule lessons.

3. Schedule all the lesson times on my calendar.

4. Adjust my budget so I will be able to afford the lessons and green fees.

5. Purchase golf clubs, shoes, and clothes.

As you think about your goals and objectives and begin to write them down, you should also consider what obstacles might come up and how you will overcome them. To avoid getting overwhelmed and discouraged, you should not attempt to accomplish too many things at one time.

If you set a goal but don't take steps to make it happen, you're not serious. Deciding to do something is not enough: you have to get up and get moving! By writing your goals and objectives down, your priorities are clearer. You'll be more effective at achieving them because you'll be working on the right things.

Is It Worth Your Time?

No matter what you do, you will only have 24/7 and 52 weeks a year to do it. You can't borrow a couple of hours from Tuesday and move it to Thursday so you will have to guard your time as if it is gold. Situations will arise that tempt you away from your work; think about the impact such distractions will have on meeting your goals. Only after a careful evaluation should you make a decision to do it or not.

You also need to consider what you want to spend your time doing. And most important, how do you want to spend your free time?

The activities in the following time log represent things you have to do, not chores that are optional (e.g., cleaning out the refrigerator). Log your daily activities to determine how much free time you have every week.

Find Free Time

Weekly Activities	Daily Hrs	#Days Per Wk	Wkly Hrs
Hours spent working at a job	10	X5	= 50
Hours spent in class	0	X?	=
Hours spent preparing for bed & sleep	8	X7	= 56
Time spent getting dressed	1.5	X6	= 9
Time spent dressing others	0	X7	=
Time spent commuting to/from work	1	X5	= 5
Time spent commuting to/from school	0	X?	=
Time spent cooking/eating food	2	X7	= 14
		TOTAL	134

DO THE MATH - With 168 hrs/wk

```
  168
- 134.0  Less hours I use
= 34.0  Total of free hours
```

Make choices that will help you
reach your goals, and also choose activities
that will make you happy.

My Free Time
How I Will Use It

Personal	Business
❑ Spending more time with family and friends.	❑ Learning more about my job or business.
❑ Watching favorite TV shows.	❑ Learning more about my industry.
❑ Hanging out.	❑ Learning more about my clients.
❑ Talking on phone.	
❑ Partying.	❑ Investing time in learning more technology.
❑ Shopping.	
❑ Looking for stuff instead of organizing it.	❑ Looking for stuff instead of organizing it.
❑ Playing video games.	❑ Reading for knowledge.
❑ Playing sports.	❑ Building relationships with people who can help me get to the next level.
❑ Sending/reading jokes and other junk in e-mail.	
❑ Spending time with people that I don't enjoy being with.	❑ Sending/reading jokes and other junk in e-mail.

Continued...

My Free Time
How I Will Use It

Personal	Business
❑ Counseling friends/gossiping.	❑ Doing extra work for recognition.
❑ Spending more time on a hobby.	❑ Interacting with people who help motivate me.
❑ Dating.	❑ Improving skills I'm not strong in, such as writing, presenting, etc.
❑ Mindless surfing (the Internet).	
❑ Participating in religious activities.	
❑ Exercising and getting fit.	OTHER ❑
❑ Continuing relationships with people who don't share a positive outlook.	❑
	❑
❑ Reading for pleasure.	❑
❑ Volunteering in the community.	❑

When making decisions about your daily activities, you have to ask yourself: Is this task or service worth giving up my free time? And is this a personal choice? Remember—how you spend your time determines your quality of life. (See graphic on next page.)

Establish Priorities

If you spend too much time on fun, easy, low-value work instead of important work, you won't be very effective. Since everything cannot be done first, you will have to develop a system to prioritize tasks.

☺ Organize what needs to be done. If you've followed the advice in this book, you have already organized your materials and can think more clearly. You should apply the same methodology to completing your work: instead of spreading it out over your desk and floor, batch related work into folders. If you are working on a complex project, use a binder with tabs to keep similar documentation together.

☺ Develop a strategy to get the work done. Make a list of everything you are working on so you'll have a clearer sense of what you are doing and why.

  ☺ Determine if the work is actually needed. Find out if you are spending time on work that adds no value (e.g., a report that no one reads).

  ☺ Estimate how much time each task or project will take (not necessarily in hours/minutes

TIP Is it Worth it? You Decide.

☀ Natasha and Felicia decided to go in together and buy bulk quantities of items such as paper towels, napkins, and toiletries, at the local membership warehouse. They spent 30 minutes on the phone talking about it and coordinating their schedules. They met up, went to the warehouse, and shopped for about two hours. When they got back to their cars, they spent another 30 minutes separating their purchases. In the end, Natasha and Felicia each spent over three hours of their free time and they saved about $22.00 each.

☀ Philip is a consultant. His new corporate client processed his paycheck and told Philip he was about to put it in the mail. Though he knew how busy this client was, Philip wanted to get as much face time with him as he could. He said he

Continued...

TIP Is it Worth it? You Decide.

would pick up the check. It took about two hours, in traffic, for Philip to reach the client's office. By the time he went through security to get into the building, another 15 minutes had passed. His check was at the reception desk and his client was not available. As he was sitting in traffic driving back to his own office, Philip realized that he had spent over two hours of his free time to just say hello to the receptionist who had his check.

✵ Jeremy needs to get some computer graphics created. He knows he could pay someone to do this at a fraction of the cost of his time. But when Jeremy can switch from his executive role and do something creative it soothes his soul.

but something general such as Quick, Long, Longer, Longest).

⊕ Determine the resources you need. If you need help from a co-worker who is tied up on another task, you may have to postpone this project.

⊕ Write a brief description of how you rationalized each item in the plan.

⊕ **Understand how one thing affects others.** If you let one project or task deadline slip, or you are not doing work in the right sequential order, you should know how that will affect other schedules and deadlines you (and others) have in place.

For instance, you have a training manual that needs to be at the printer at least thirty days before the class in order to get it printed, bound, and shipped. What would happen if you failed to count backward from the due date and didn't leave enough time to get the job done?

Do the most important work first. Activities that bring in the highest revenues the soonest will keep you employed or in business. Consequently, you should assign a project's importance based on how it relates to the bottom line (whatever *you* think this is should match management's opinion, so always ask to ensure clarification).

For example, you should do a proposal for a current client before a proposal for a potential client (a current client is closer to the bottom line than one you have not yet worked with).

Mark each task or project on a scale of A-B-C with A being the most important. Now review this list again and put another A, B, or C next to each item. Then repeat, putting another A, B, or C next to each item. Always bear in mind—activities that will help you achieve your goals should have a higher priority.

These high-priority tasks are ones you will not delegate.

NOTE Later in this book, you will discover how to streamline work processes and incorporate technology solutions to speed everything up. Projects that are taking you too long now will get done much faster.

Prioritizing Tasks and Projects

Project/Task	Priority	Explanation	Time frame	Re-sources
Project H	AAA	Hot! Do now.	Quick	None
Project I	AAA	Hot! Do today. Will take some time to do. Re-arrange workload and schedule this now to work on today and tomorrow.	Long	None
Task J	A	Important. Schedule it and do in a few days.	Longer	Proof-reader
Project K	AA	Urgent and important but not hot. Do within a couple of days after checking with resources. The researcher will need to get started at least 2 weeks before the writer.	Longest	Writer, researcher

Continued...

Prioritizing
Tasks and Projects

Project/Task	Priority	Explanation	Time frame	Re- sources
Project L	BB	Important but not urgent. Long-term project; will map out a plan next week. Schedule 2 hours next week to get started.	Longest	Don't know yet
Project M	B	This isn't important right now but it might be later. Need to explore possibilities. Delegate.	Long	Dele- gate to Joe
Task N	CC	Not important but get it over with because I dread doing it. Do it now.	Quick	None
Task P	CCC	Not important and doesn't matter when it gets done. Put in tickler file for next month.	Longer	None
Task R	X	No one reads this report. Stop doing it.		

Say No Without the Guilt

Once your goals are set, you want to stay focused on what's important. You must learn how to say no.

You probably don't like to say no because it makes you feel guilty. But when you say yes—and then could kick yourself later—you feel worse. Why are you the one always getting asked? It could be that your name is at the top of the list. Or it could be that you have established the reputation of being an easy yes. When someone asks for your help and you know you can't oblige, you will have to gather all your strength and say no. The key is in how you say it.

To assuage your guilt over saying no, take these four steps:

1. Acknowledge the request as if you would like to help.

2. Say "No" but maintain a pleasant facial expression.

3. End your response with something positive and upbeat.

4. Remove yourself from the situation.

Instead of: "No, I can't do it."

Try this: "What a great idea! Unfortunately, I don't have the extra time to devote to such a worthwhile cause. I wish you the best with this!"

Say it and get out of there, get off the phone, or bow your head and get back to work. Resist efforts to convince you to change your mind. It will be tough to do this at first, but the more you try it the easier it will get.

Another Way to Say No

Another way to say no is to say yes first. For example: "Can you do this work for less?" Try one of these responses:

- ☺ "Yes I can, but I wouldn't be able to give your project the time needed to do a quality job and you deserve better."

- ☺ "Yes, but we won't have complete success and I'm afraid you'll be disappointed. I want you to be 100 percent satisfied."

- ☺ "Yes, but I have to maintain a certain profit margin in order to continue servicing my clients in the way they deserve."

Improvement Five:
Reduce Information Overload

Reduce the amount of information you are letting in and evaluate it as it relates to your current goals.

What is the benefit of reducing information overload?

Spending less time on information interruptions leaves you more time to accomplish and be focused on your goals.

What concepts must I understand to reduce information overload?

You need information to supplement your knowledge so that you can make better and more informed decisions. But at some point, if you aren't careful, you'll go into overload, receiving far more information than you need.

What actions must I take to reduce information overload?

Information is increasingly available from various sources and you are choosing to let it in. You must filter out what is unimportant and focus only on the core activities that will help you (and the people depending on you) reach your goals. Here are some tips on how to do that.

Build a Database of Experts

You can't know or do everything. That's why you call a plumber when your pipes burst or a mechanic when your car needs repair. You'll have to do the same thing in business. Once your goals are set and your plan outlined, to get the work done, focus on that and how to do it better. The people around you will have the expertise to supplement your skills and knowledge if you ever need it.

Consequently, if you are subscribing to newsletters, blogs, and RSS feeds that cover far more information about a topic than you need to know, unsubscribe. Or if you are a computer trainer teaching Microsoft Outlook® and questions come up in a class about Outlook® Express, instead of trying to find the answer, tell them, "I don't know, but Jackie Johnson at BDE is an expert."

Unclutter Your Mind

When you waste brain cells trying to remember everything, your thoughts can get so cluttered with dates, deadlines, and other action items that you easily get overwhelmed. Are you constantly blindsided by forgotten due dates? Are you always putting out fires instead of being prepared? Are you hanging up the phone feeling embarrassed because someone had to remind you of a commitment you made but forgot about?

A cluttered mind (just like a cluttered office) reduces your productivity and stifles your creativity. You might be getting a lot done but at what cost? Write the answer to the following question and read it every day: "What do I want to have more time to do?"

External Cues Help You Remember

When you rely too much on your memory, you can easily forget many important details. Relying on memory is stressful, too. A better solution is to use external cues to help you remember.

NOTE Use your brain for thinking, not for remembering.

⊕ Calendar. Anything that is going to occur during your day should be noted on your calendar. Whether it's a board meeting, your son's baseball game, a PTA meeting, or a neighborhood gathering, write it down. If you have work on your to-do list that is going to take blocks of time to complete, note that on your calendar, too.

- ⊕ **To-do list.** Get everything out of your head. Regardless of how small or trivial the task, write it down or note it electronically. Depending on what the task is, you might have to do both! Once it's recorded, it's off your mind but you won't forget it. Check off the items you complete and highlight the ones you don't.

- ⊕ **Voice recorder.** When you are driving, use a voice-activated recorder to send yourself reminders. You probably have this feature on your cell phone or PDA. A free service at www.jott.com converts your voice into e-mails, text messages, reminders, lists, and appointments.

- ⊕ **Follow-up file.** Instead of leaving documents in a pile in plain view as a so-called reminder, use some type of tickler file. Put the paperwork in the appropriate time slot and schedule time

on your calendar to do the work. (These tickler files, sometimes referred to as an everyday file, have slots for every date of the month, for every month of the year. They can be purchased at any major office supply store.)

- ④ **Computer reminders.** Have your computer remind you to check your tickler file every day.

- ④ **Checklists.** Use checklists if you need to remember a list of things (e.g., for travel or a meeting).

- ④ **Project folders.** If you are working on a complex project, use a binder with tabs to keep similar documentation together (e.g., a conference planning notebook with tabs for Administration, Exhibitors, Logistics, Marketing, Speakers, Sponsors).

- ④ **Password manager.** If you have trouble remembering all the passwords you have set up at different web sites, try an online vault such as www.PassPack.com. You can store passwords, Frequent Flyer miles, registration numbers, whatever you want, and access this information from anywhere you have Internet access. The password to this site is the only one you will have to remember.

- ④ **Electronic notes.** Throughout the day, you'll make notes, find tips, receive instructions, etc., that you'll want to keep track of. There are several options for keeping this miscellaneous information, but to make it searchable, store it electronically.

- ⊕ www.EverNote.com. This technology captures information (in various formats) and makes it accessible and searchable on your computer, PDA, mobile phone, and the Web.

- ⊕ **Document information with hyperlinks to bookmarked text that is categorized based on the topic**. Or you could use a word processing document with a table of contents based on heading levels that is set up to hyperlink to the desired page.

- ⊕ **Address book**. Your electronic address book does more than just store contact information for people: You can use it to keep track of miscellaneous notes. Create a "contact" for anything you need access to quickly, using the text area for notes. It will always be at your fingertips (and synched to your PDA). Make sure to give each "contact" a logical name so you can locate it quickly later.

Contacts

Contact Name	Description
Airlines	Keep a list of airlines you use and include links to their web sites and phone numbers, your frequent flyer numbers, airport codes to use online, etc.
Computer	Use this contact to list information about your computer, such as the order number/date of purchase, service code/tag (the manufacturer will ask for this if you call for service), warranty expiration date (put this on your calendar also), and open ticket numbers along with notes, which come in handy if you make a lot of service calls.
Write about this	If you write a lot, keep article ideas here.

E-mail Overload

E-mail overload happens when your Inbox becomes packed with hundreds or thousands of messages you no longer need.

Most of these messages could have been deleted upon arrival or immediately after you read them. The remaining ones (representing unfinished work, requests for your time, missed deadlines, and broken promises) should have been handled and then filed or deleted.

To get your Inbox under control, you'll have to trim it down to one screen and then commit to keeping it that way.

Make Companywide Changes

Larger organizations tend to have a bigger problem with e-mail overload than smaller ones. The load could be reduced if the company were to change its e-mail culture.

- Address bad e-mail habits.

  - Distribute on a need-to-know basis. Send your messages to the right people and only Reply All when it is necessary.

  - Write descriptive subject lines. The e-mail subject line should read like a newspaper headline and tell the whole story. The recipient should understand what your message is about before he opens it. This also makes it easier to find later after you file it.

⊕ **Make your subject line match the message.** Don't reply to an e-mail if the new message is totally unrelated to the original message. The subject line will indicate one thing and the body of the e-mail something else. Would you send a company letter or memo out like this?

⊕ **Limit messages to one topic.** It will be easier for the recipient to prioritize and file messages if you limit them to one topic. If you do discuss various topics within one message, note that in the subject line and number each new topic in the body.

⊕ **Be thorough but brief.** Your message should be brief but contain enough information to tell the whole story. If you receive more than three messages with requests for clarification, a return phone call will work better.

⊕ **Address the message appropriately.** People on the "To" line will take action. Use the "Cc" line to copy people for information only (and only when they really need to know). Use "Bcc" when you are sending the message to a large list or sending it privately.

⊕ **Do not send acknowledgments.** If you work in a job that permits it, limit useless acknowledgments by ending your messages with

"Thanks in advance," or "NRN" which means No Response Necessary). When you receive a message, refrain from sending one-word messages to say "Thanks."

⊕ Do not send jokes, prayers, and thoughts for the day. People are busy (and you should be, too). Work is not the place for this type of e-mail.

⊕ Train your people. Most software programs have powerful, little-known features that can help everyone work more efficiently. It does little good to purchase software and not require sufficient training on how to use it.

⊕ Avoid sending routine, internal messages. Instead of sending internal communications via e-mail, add it to the Intranet and let people read it on their own.

⊕ Change expectations of immediate responses. Most employees should be allowed to send a response within 24 to 48 hours and should not be chastised for not responding immediately. In emergencies, they should use the phone.

⊕ Create a companywide classification system. Develop codes for subject lines that make the subject and required action obvious at a glance. Of course, it's important that everyone knows what the codes mean. For example:

MTG	Meeting.
AI	Action Item.
IRN	Immediate Response Needed.
NRN	No Response Necessary.
END	Use at the end of a subject line when it includes everything you had to say. No need to open message.

Change How You Use the Inbox

The Inbox is meant for temporary storage of e-mail messages. It is not intended as a long-term filing solution or to be used as follows:

- ⊙ **To-do list for unfinished work.** This information should be added to a task list, project folder, or whatever system you use to organize work you need to do.

- ⊙ **Tickler file that reminds you of work.** A better solution is to add this message to a work file with a computer reminder that will help you remember.

- ⊙ **Calendar with meeting notices and reminders.** An alternative is to put this information on your calendar and set a reminder.

- ⊙ **Database for addresses and phone numbers.** This information should be added to your address book for easy retrieval.

- ⊙ **Filing system for finished work.** It's better to create Inbox folders and file the message or you can save it somewhere else on your computer.

Organize Your Inbox and Get It to One Screen

You should organize your Inbox using the same methods as recommended for paper files: purge and set up folders using broad categories with a logical breakdown.

NOTE

Schedule a meeting with your Inbox and empty it.

YOUR GOAL: To always see the bottom of your Inbox without scrolling.

You may need a few hours to clean out the current mess so go ahead and schedule this time on your calendar. Otherwise, every time you scroll through those hundreds (or thousands) of messages, you'll be thinking: "Call Joe, forgot that meeting, what does she need?, oops, I forgot about that, huh?, call Maurice, don't have time to do this, report is due, what the heck is this?, customer needs help, I need help, *#!!?…" On the other hand, once you have a clean, organized Inbox, you'll be motivated to delete most messages or put them in the right place and deal with them at an appropriate time.

Consider the following as you review each message and delete everything you can.

⊙ Do it if it's quick or schedule time to do it later. If you can do the work in two to three minutes, go ahead. Otherwise, schedule time on your calendar, create a task, or make a note on your to-do list to handle it later.

- ⊕ **File it if you need to keep it.** Save the message in one of your Inbox folders or somewhere else on your computer.

- ⊕ **Pend it and wait.** You pend work when you need information that someone else has or you are waiting on someone to do their part. Create a pending folder as part of your Inbox filing system and add the message there.

- ⊕ **Follow up on it later.** Move the message into whatever tracking system you use and set a date to follow up on it.

- ⊕ **Delegate it then follow up.** Get others to do the work by delegating it appropriately. Add the request to whatever system you use to track work.

- ⊕ **Print it only if you must.** Don't print messages unless you have to take them with you and keeping them electronically is not an option.

Establish a Routine to Keep E-mail Under Control

You don't have to be available the instant a new e-mail message arrives. If it's that important, the sender should call. You should establish a routine for checking e-mail that best fits your schedule and the type of work you do. Experiment with when and how often you need to check it until you find the right fit for you.

Voicemail Overload

With the popularity of e-mail, voicemail may not be as much of a problem for you as it used to be. But if it is, you can manage it better by adjusting some of your habits and improving how you use the technology (so keep the instructions under your phone).

Incoming Calls

⊕ **Improve your outgoing message.** Let callers know when they will hear back from you. If you're going to be out of the office for an extended period, update your message with your status (some people do this every day).

Add the following to your outgoing message:

⊕ Ask that they leave a subject so you will be prepared for the return call.

⊕ Remind them to speak slowly when leaving their phone number and to include their extension if they have one.

⊕ Ask them to send an e-mail message in case you are traveling.

⊕ Refer them to your web site, which should have helpful information callers routinely request.

⊕ **Don't make promises you can't keep.** If you receive more calls than you can possibly return, stop saying that you will, as in: "Please leave a message and I'll call you back as soon as I can." If you work in a service organization where you field a lot of "generic" calls, change your message to something such as: "Please listen to this entire message. Due to the number of calls I receive, I cannot return all of them, but I do want to help you. Our web site has been updated, and you will most likely find your answers there. If not, the best way to contact me is by e-mail at myemail@xyz123.com."

⊕ **Don't ask people to call.** If your job requires a lot of networking or people are clamoring to get to you, be more selective about casually mentioning to people that they should contact you. If you aren't interested in their offering and have no intention of returning their call, don't waste their time by asking them to get in touch. Practice techniques you've already learned: Just say "no" or refer them to your web site.

⊕ **Forward to voicemail automatically.** When you need to stay focused and a ringing phone distracts you, forward it to voicemail or use your Do Not Disturb button if your phone system has one.

⊕ **Answer via e-mail.** When the information the caller needs is not complex, you can avoid idle chatter by answering via e-mail when appropriate.

⊕ **Monitor requests and offer alternatives.** You should spend some time thinking about common requests you get from callers. Perhaps you could add more details to your web site or make sure the information is easy to navigate to, or refer callers to more appropriate extensions based on their requests (e.g., directions to your office), or use autoresponders that can send specific information via fax or e-mail.

⊕ **Schedule a time to check.** Instead of constantly checking voicemail throughout the day, designate a specific time to check it and block that time on your calendar to return calls. Use some type of log as you listen to your messages, either a separate notebook or your to-do book.

Outgoing Calls

⊕ **Set special numbers up in speed dial.** Record numbers you dial most often into the speed dial keys, including the number you call to check voicemail.

⊕ **Go right to the beep.** Phone companies use different shortcuts for bypassing an outgoing message and going right to the beep (try #, *, or 1). Once you find out what it is, add the shortcut to your address book for each contact.

⊕ **Get to a live person.** You have undoubtedly experienced Interactive Voice Response (IVR), also known as "voicemail jail," or those loops with a computer recording rather than a live person. With the right code, you can either get to a real person or get in the queue to wait for one. First try pressing "0" for the operator (you may have to press "0" several times). If that doesn't work, try the list of codes for 500 of the largest companies at www.GetHuman.com.

- ⊕ **Leave good messages.** When leaving messages:

  1. Say your name first (spell it if it is some-thing other than Smith).

  2. Say your phone number slowly and include your extension (regardless of whether you think they have it or not).

  3. Leave a brief message.

  4. Slowly repeat your phone number and ex-tension before you hang up.

- ⊕ **Use a list to keep you on point.** It's easy to stray from the intended purpose of a call. A simple outline will help you stay on track. If it is a type of call you make often, create a checklist.

NOTE

> When you leave your phone number, say it as if you are writing it down because that is what someone will do when they listen to your message. Don't assume your number is showing up in Caller ID.

Postal Mail Overload

Deal with the mail as it comes in instead of allowing it to pile up. Just because someone sent you something doesn't mean you have to keep it, so process your mail near a shredder and waste basket.

- Set up a special place for mail to go. Establish a place for the mail to go such as an INBOX (somewhere other than on your desk), a hanging file over a door, etc. Separate the mail by recipient and keep bills together.

- Establish a routine to process mail. Create folders to batch similar work such as TO DO, TO PAY, TO RESPOND, TO COPY. Trash or shred everything else as you open it.

- Keep only what you value. Don't keep anything that has no use or value or if it is information you can get somewhere else.

- Respond quickly. When appropriate, send a quick, handwritten note on a preprinted card, write a response directly on the letter, send an e-mail message, or call. Avoid sending formal responses that must go through several rounds of approvals.

- Use a routing slip to distribute to others. If you work in a larger organization, use a routing slip to distribute mail to other staff.

ROUTING REQUEST	From:
Phone/e-mail:	

TO:

❑	❑	❑
❑	❑	❑
❑	❑	❑
❑	❑	❑
❑	❑	❑
❑ Other Recipients		

PLEASE:

❑ Call ❑ Copy ❑ Fax ❑ Mail ❑ Sched. ❑ Type ❑ Write

	DUE:	COMMENTS:
❑ Handle-Review w/me by		
❑ Handle by due date of		
❑ Review with me. Call for appt. by		
❑ Read - pass on - Last reader back to me		
❑ Read - pass on - Last reader recycle or trash		
❑ Read - back to me		
❑ Read – no need to return to me		

In a big company environment, the mail can pile up quickly, especially for busy executives. If you're procrastinating about dealing with it and work is slipping, change how you handle it.

If you're fortunate enough to have a personal assistant, the two of you should create a routine and spend time together every possible day to keep your Inbox and Outbox empty. Have him or her process your mail, not just give it to you.

TIP *The Executive's Mail*

The Assistant should:

❑ **Prioritize mail with folders.** Mail should be separated into colored folders for ACTION, READ, MISCELLANEOUS READ, SIGNATURE, and TO PAY.

❑ **Highlight important points.** Scan the material and highlight any important points and due dates.

❑ **Pull any referenced material.** If the document references any previous correspondence or mailings, pull them and attach them (only use jumbo paper clips so everything stays together).

❑ **Delegate mail when it arrives.** If you know the executive will delegate the work to a manager or staffer, you should do it. Write a note on the top page with the date it should be back to you, make a copy of the top page only, and place it in your tickler file as a reminder.

Continued...

TIP The Executive's Mail

❏ **Follow up later to ensure all due dates are met.** Your job is to ensure all deadlines are met. Check your tickler or task list every day (create a computer reminder to check it).

The Executive should:
❏ **Establish a routine for processing.** You and your assistant should process the mail together at a mutually agreeable time, (try to establish a regular time). *This will make your job easier because it will help your assistant:*

- Learn the business
- Understand how you think and handle various situations
- Handle things for you
- Keep you posted on new developments

❏ **Give good instructions.** As you review the mail together, give clear instructions and insist that the assistant take good notes.

Improvement Six:
Manage Interruptions

Keep distractions at bay so you can focus on what's most important.

What is the benefit of managing interruptions?

Reducing distractions—both internal (from yourself) and external (from others)—will help you take control of your time.

What concepts must I understand to manage interruptions?

After every interruption, it takes five to ten minutes to regroup. Some interruptions can't be avoided (for instance, say a co-worker becomes ill); some can be postponed (a ringing phone during a meeting); and some are the nature of the job (calls received by a help desk analyst on call). But for many others, you can make changes in your environment and work habits that will prevent workflow disruptions.

What actions must I take to effectively manage interruptions?

To keep interruptions to a minimum, you will have to change your workspace and your work habits.

Change Your Workspace

- Get organized. Clutter reduces people's confidence in you so they'll continue to interrupt you for updates. It also distracts you. Every time you sit down to work, something in a pile will catch your eye and your attention so you continue to interrupt yourself.

- Rearrange office furniture. Arrange your office so that you won't be tempted to make eye contact with every person who passes by. If you look up and your eyes lock, they'll visit. You should also reduce the number of chairs you have for visitors, and make sure the ones you do have aren't too comfortable.

- Reduce the lighting. Turn off your overhead light and use a desk lamp so it will look like you're not in your office.

- Remove toys and candy. If you have a game on display or a jar of candy, you're asking for a visit.

- Create a "busy signal." Let your team know when you need to stay focused. You could close your door or hang a sign on your cubicle.

Change Your Habits

⊕ Stop the 9-1-1 mentality. You don't have to be available for every call, e-mail, or instant message just as it arrives. Stay focused on important work that requires your total concentration and create a routine for responding to everything else.

24-7 Connectivity

Receptionists, specialists on call for medical emergencies, 9-1-1 operators, and high-level technicians on call have to answer calls the moment they arrive. But why do you?

Do you have to be involved with every detail? Everyone on your team has a job function and should be trained well enough to make good decisions based on well-thought-out processes and procedures. If this is the case and you still don't trust your people to do their jobs, you either need to change your management style or you need some new people.

Would you get chastised if responses are not immediate? Let management know that you prefer to stay focused on what is most important. If you have developed routines that drive more business or make their jobs easier, the results of those efforts will show.

Are you addicted? Do you sleep with your gadgets under your pillow?

Continued...

24-7 Connectivity

If you aren't concentrating on anything long enough to do a job well, how will you reach your goals? Perhaps you need to box up your PDA or cell phone and ship it to yourself using 3-day ground. You'll begin to get used to being without it.

Do you feel that it takes less time to answer a call immediately than to return the call or send a reply later? You are interrupting important activities to deal with something that may not be. Stay focused and set aside a time to handle the interruption later.

Are you bored with your job or business? Does staying connected give you something to do? If you invested that extra time you have in learning something new, you would become more competitive in the marketplace.

Do you think that if you do not talk to a caller immediately, you might not get another chance? Consider sending an e-mail message instead to set up a time to talk.

- ① Do not multitask. When you multitask you are actually interrupting yourself. Instead of staying focused on finishing one task, you start one project, jump over to another, answer the phone, check your e-mail, get a cup of coffee, and so on. A better practice is to either finish what you're doing or get to a good stopping point before moving to something else. On the other hand, if you're working on something that doesn't require much thought, you can probably handle a quick interruption without getting off track.

- ① Avoid instant messaging (IM). If real-time interaction doesn't add high value to your communication, why are you so glued to it? Rethink how you are allowing this constant interruption to keep you from more important work.

- ① Respect other people's time. If you like to visit co-workers when you're not busy, don't expect them to honor your need to be left alone when you are.

- ① Don't become the in-house librarian for facts, figures, and files. Encourage everyone to maintain their own systems so they can find what they need when they need it.

- ① Reduce personal phone calls. Take note of the number of personal phone calls you receive and what they are about. Either ask people not to call you during work hours unless it's an emergency, or don't answer the phone when you can't talk (that includes cell phone calls). If you get a lot of calls from family members looking for things, it's well past time for everyone to get organized.

- ⊕ Train employees sufficiently. The more you invest in training your employees, the fewer questions they'll have. For this to make a difference, you will need well-defined processes and procedures for everyone to follow.

- ⊕ Delegate it properly. If you invest sufficient time giving an overview of a project and supplying your staff with clear instructions, they shouldn't need to come back for clarification later.

Change How You Handle Your Co-workers

- ⊕ Examine your open-door policy. Somehow, an open-door policy came to mean that employees can just stroll into any office at any time. Not quite. An effective open-door policy makes it clear that employees should first attempt to solve problems or share ideas with their immediate managers (after scheduling the time). Then, if they aren't satisfied, they can elevate their concerns up the chain of command without repercussions. Consequently, you should feel free to close your door when you need uninterrupted time.

- ⊕ Set up regular meetings. Instead of constantly calling, sending e-mail messages, or stopping by someone's office to discuss items that aren't crucial, set up regular (and short) meetings. Ask everyone to create folders to keep items to be discussed at the next meeting.

- ⊕ Develop a script for unannounced visitors. When someone interrupts you, let them know

---

immediately that you don't have the time. Say something such as, "Denise, I understand that you need to see me about your report and I'm eager to hear about it, but I need to spend the next couple of hours working on this project. I have some free time tomorrow morning. How about 9 o'clock? Or can it just wait until our regular meeting this week?" Be firm. You have important work to do.

🕐 **Stand up to talk to drop-ins.** Visitors won't stay long if you stand up and glance at your watch as they come in. If they don't get the hint, it might be a good time to take a bio break. Head toward the door and ask them to talk to you on the way.

🕐 **Use voicemail.** Don't answer the phone when you don't have time to talk. When you're working on something important or meeting with someone, forward your phone to voicemail. You can return all calls later at a regularly scheduled time.

Last Minute?

Improvement Seven:
Stop Procrastinating

Start your work now so you'll have enough time to do it right.

What is the benefit of ending procrastination?

Giving yourself enough time guarantees that you'll do your best work.

What concepts must I understand to stop procrastinating?

You can replace the bad habit of procrastinating with the good habit of doing the work. To break the bad habit, you'll have to get as creative in coming up with ideas of how to get the work done as you have been in thinking up reasons not to do it. Plan ahead and get everything you need to complete the job, including acquiring the right skills.

What actions must I take to stop procrastinating?

There are several possible reasons Jason procrastinated about doing this report.

TIP

Sweating up to the Last Minute

Jason was directed to write a report on how his department could improve its customer service next year. He had plenty of time to get the project done; he figured he could put it off until later. But he did leave the project folder on top of one of his piles as a reminder.

Jason looked at that folder, every day for two weeks, and every time he did, the thought of doing the work nagged at him. By week three the folder had gotten buried under other work. He came across the folder one day while looking for a letter. He glanced at it, but figured he still had plenty of time to get it done. Back in the pile it went.

More days passed. Suddenly the report was due the next day. For weeks, Jason had concocted every reason he could think of for avoiding the project, and now he knew he would be up all night working on it. He'll sweat right up to the last minute and will hand in an inferior report.

- He thinks he works best when waiting until the last minute. This is a myth. If Jason likes the rush he gets at the last minute, he should find more positive ways to experience that excitement. This method simply ensures that he'll never be able to do his best work because he'll always run out of time.

- He wonders if he is the best person to do the work. Jason might not be very confident about his writing abilities, so the thought of having to write a report makes him miserable. He also might not be his department's customer service expert, or be very creative when it comes to developing new ideas.

  It's common to procrastinate over things that you lack the confidence to do. Jason could have delegated this project to someone on his staff better suited to it. He could also enroll in a writing class to improve his skills.

- He saw the task as huge and overwhelming. By breaking the project up into smaller, more manageable parts and setting deadlines for each phase, Jason could have viewed the task much differently.

  Setting deadlines, even when you're working on a project alone, gives you a goal to work toward. Make a commitment to yourself or someone else to review the work by a certain date.

This will help you get started and will keep you motivated.

- He wasn't familiar with technology that could make the job easier. Computer software can perform magic. If Jason knew how to use the right software in the right way, he could complete his work much faster. He could set up a template that would make it easy to create the report and then update it. He could also import files from other departments, or create charts or graphs that would help explain his ideas.

⊕ He doesn't particularly like writing reports. Jason might not like every aspect of his job, but he still has to do his best at everything. He shouldn't have spent his valuable time agonizing over doing the work; instead he simply should have scheduled time on his calendar to get it done and off his mind. And doing the most dreadful tasks first thing in the morning would mean that the rest of his day would be even better.

⊕ He isn't as organized as he needs to be. Jason had been thinking all year about ways to improve customer service. He jotted down ideas on sticky notes, various note pads, dinner napkins, and anything else that was nearby when he had an idea. But when he needed all these scraps he couldn't find them. He had even pulled some great articles together that would help spur his creativity, but he had no idea where those were. If Jason had set up a Customer Service Ideas file earlier in the year, he could have used it to collect all this useful information.

⊕ He isn't busy enough. Jason might not have had enough work to do and had gotten bored. A busy person working on the right things in the right way gets things done. As they say: The more you have to do, the more you get done.

TIP   How to Change a Habit, Step by Step

A habit is defined as something done often, easily, and without thought. If you want to change a habit, you have to change your thoughts (it can take up to twenty-one days to change a habit).

1. Write down the habit you want to change (e.g., *stop putting my car keys just anywhere when I get home*).

2. Write the date you want to begin changing the habit on your calendar (e.g., *start today*). Mark the 21st day from the time you start.

3. Commit to making the change by telling someone who will encourage you not to give up.

4. Before you get out of your car and walk into the house, think about where you have decided to put your keys.

Continued...

TIP
How to Change a Habit, Step by Step

5. Walk into your house and put your keys in that place.

6. Repeat Steps 4 and 5 every day when you get home until you put your keys in your special place without thinking about it. On the days you do forget, get back into your car and complete Steps 4 and 5.

7. Once you've realized success—putting your keys in your special place without thought—reward yourself!

Note: If after twenty-one days you're still not quite there, reassess what techniques worked well and when, and then identify the changes you still need to make. Take them one step and one habit at a time until you realize success.

Improvement Eight:
Streamline Processes

Examine how you are currently working and develop better, faster ways to get everything done.

What is the benefit of streamlining processes?

Thinking things through, as opposed to diving in without a plan, saves time and effort.

What concepts must I understand to streamline processes?

A process can be defined as a routine for handling a task. It is definable, can be mapped out, and is repeatable. Instead of continuing to do the work the way you always have, ask yourself:

 ⊕ Why am I doing this?

 ⊕ Why am I doing it like this?

 ⊕ Can technology make this easier?

What actions must I take to streamline processes?

People often choose working harder over taking the time to figure out how to work smarter.

Create a Process

If some items on your to-do list are really projects rather than tasks, move them to your calendar and schedule time to get them done. Before you dig in, think everything through and develop the best approach.

Here is a simple way to construct a process for one of your work assignments.

Streamlining Processes

Get Started	Think It Through
☐ List everything that needs to be done	No matter how trivial the task is, get it out of your head by writing it down or keeping it electronically. For each task, name it and determine what the outcome needs to be.
☐ Examine every task	Is it necessary? Can you streamline it? How can technology make it easier? If you have done this type of project before, which part of it took more time than you believe it should have? Think this through to determine better ways to handle it. If a task seems large and overwhelming, break it into smaller parts.
☐ Check with others involved	If other people will be involved with any phase of a project, check in with them. Ask: "What can I do

Continued...

Streamlining Processes

Get Started	Think It Through
	on my end that will make it easier for you on your end?" Also check their availability throughout the project.
❏ Prioritize each item	Group similar tasks and arrange them in the right sequential order. (Use something as simple as sticky notes to record them and move items around until you develop a logical flow.) Arrange tasks based on importance and the time it will take to get each done. (For example, say you have a request that is not a priority, but will take days to get a response. Go ahead and request this information in the beginning so you'll have it when you need it.)

Continued...

Streamlining Processes

Get Started	Think It Through
❏ Determine supplies, equipment, etc., you will need	For any job, you need the right tools. Keep a list of tools nearby so you won't forget.
❏ Organize your project files	Determine the best way to keep all the information related to your project together (instead of scattering the documents all over your desk).
❏ Set up a schedule	Create a timeline, start with the due date and work backward to make sure you have time to do the work.
❏ Put a tracking system in place	To keep you on schedule, use a tracking system appropriate to the project (e.g., Outlook tasks, a project notebook, your planner).

Continued...

Streamlining Processes

Get Started	Think It Through
☐ Review use of technology	Continue to review tasks to determine if technology can make any of them easier. Ask an expert if you're not sure.
☐ Document the process	Create written instructions for every phase of the project. Write them so that anyone could follow them, even if you aren't available.

Process Example

Create and streamline a process for setting up and conducting Webinars (*seminars given via the Internet*).

(Similar tasks are grouped and listed as they need to happen)

Action	ACTION PLAN – Step by Step
❏ Set Up	1. Finalize dates with instructors.
	2. Schedule on work calendar.
	3. Schedule on public web calendar.
	4. Add dates to online registration form.
	5. Schedule web conference center.
	- Assign password.
	- Note class code.
	- Note class type/name.

Continued...

Process Example

Action	ACTION PLAN – Step by Step
☐ Promote and Remind	1. Alert members of new dates. 2. Write a promotional script and save as template. 3. Send via e-mail at regular intervals. 4. Remind instructors.
☐ Conduct Training	1. Download registrations and create roster. 2. Send registrants all registration codes, handouts, and other instructions via e-mail. 3. Perform action on specified date.
☐ Close Out	1. Send evaluations. 2. Tally evaluation results. 3. Send results to instructors and management. 4. Submit paperwork to pay instructors.

In *reviewing the actions, determine the following*:

- ① Is the task necessary or just something you have always done?

- ① How and when will each task be performed?

- ① Which tasks need further clarification?

- ① Is there a way to computerize any tasks?

Now that you've taken sufficient time to think through the process, you have increased your chances of success. You'll also find the work less stressful. This is the point at which you should document your process and instructions. Remember to make them clear and complete so that anyone could follow them, even if you aren't available.

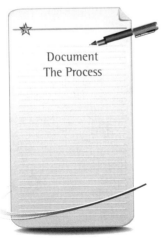

Document
The Process

Clarifying Process

Issues that Need Clarifying

How will the class data for each Webinar be captured (e.g., *password, class code, etc.*)?	**Initial Solution** Create a form providing spaces for each piece of data that needs to be collected.
	Final Solution with More Technology Create a spreadsheet using sorts and filters as needed.
Where will the information be kept (filed)? Your solution should also consider if it needs to be mobile and if others need to access it.	**Initial Solution** Create a folder and keep in workstation tray for easy access, separating the checklist from the class data.
	Final Solution with More Technology Sync the spreadsheet to your PDA so it goes wherever you go. If others need access, either place on the company server or online. *Continued...*

Clarifying Process

**Issues that
Need Clarifying**

How will you remember all of the action steps and dates (e.g., *notify instructors, when to send promotional e-mail, when to send instructions to attendees*)?	**Initial Solution** Create a checklist that lists each action.
	Final Solution with More Technology Keep the checklist as is and set up computer reminders.
What information needs to be in the e-mail to the registrants (e.g., *password, phone number*)?	**Initial Solution** Create a one-sheeter with all necessary information.
	Final Solution with More Technology Create an e-mail signature with all this info and paste it into the body of the e-mail notice.

Continued...

Clarifying Process

Issues that Need Clarifying

How will you notify the instructors? Should others be able to view the information?	**Initial Solution** Information not to be shared with others. Send individual, personalized e-mail messages.
	Final Solution with More Technology Use mail merge with data from the spreadsheet. Each instructor receives his or her info only. Create a macro that will do this with the click of a button.
How will you handle evaluations?	**Initial Solution** Send each registrant an evaluation form to complete. Print and compile results.
	Final Solution with More Technology Create online evaluation and use spreadsheet formulas to tabulate results. *Continued...*

Clarifying Process

Issues that Need Clarifying		
How will you distribute evaluation results?	**Initial Solution** E-mail to instructors and management.	
	Final Solution with More Technology Mail merge an e-mail personalized to each.	
How are instructors paid?	**Initial Solution** Submit payroll form to bookkeeper.	
	Final Solution with More Technology Use mail merge pulling data from same spreadsheet to create a payroll form that can be e-mailed to the bookkeeper. Create a macro that will do this.	

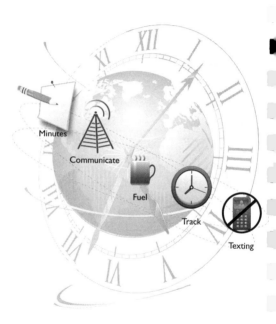

Minutes

Communicate

Fuel

Track

Texting

Improvement Nine:
Run Better Meetings

Spend only the necessary time in meetings in order to reach conclusions.

What is the benefit of running better meetings?

Ensures that there is value gained from pulling everyone away from work.

What concepts must I understand to run better meetings?

Many meetings waste time and lower employee productivity simply because of how they are convened and conducted. A study quoted in the *Wall Street Journal* estimated that American managers could save eighty percent of the time they currently waste in meetings if they start and stop on time and if they follow an agenda.

What actions must I take to run better meetings?

See the following TIP for a real life example.

TIP *Show Me the Money*

Ann is the executive assistant to the CEO. She's anxious for him to get off the phone so his weekly staff meeting can start. His meetings never begin (or end) on time. Here is what she did to coax him (and others) to change their meeting ways.

Hang clocks everywhere.

- A large clock on the CEO's wall so that he is aware of the time all day.

- Two clocks in the conference room. On one side, the facilitator and late arrivals always have a clear sense of the time. The clock on the other side keeps the attendees on track.

- All over the building so that everyone is on the same schedule.

Do the math. Ann created a breakdown of executive salaries into minutes. This figure was multiplied by the 25 minutes

Continued...

TIP Show Me the Money

executives usually sat waiting for meetings to begin, plus the 45 minutes meetings usually ran over. She was able to show the CEO how much extra money this weekly meeting was costing the company.

Make the results visual. A picture is worth a thousand words, so Ann presented her information visually with a colorful chart.

Time Wasted in Meetings This Week
Meeting Objectives Were Not Met

10 HRS

6 HRS

4 HRS

$32,390.50

Before the Meeting

Meeting Request Form

If one of your responsibilities is to schedule space, catering, audio-visual equipment, etc., for small meetings at work, a meeting request form will help ensure that you don't forget anything.

⊕ **Explore options other than face-to-face meetings.** Before you schedule your next meeting, will an e-mail message, teleconference, or Internet conference work for you? It's not always necessary to do face-to-face meetings.

⊕ **Avoid unplanned meetings as much as possible.** Your staff or co-workers have planned their day based on what they already know. Calling impromptu meetings to discuss noncritical issues is not a good use of their time or yours.

⊕ **Invite people on a need-to-know basis.** People who attend the meeting for information purposes only could read the minutes instead (or record the meeting so they can listen later).

⊕ **Reschedule the meeting if all the key people cannot attend.** You won't make much progress if your major contributors aren't there; you'll just end up having another meeting on the same topic.

⊕ **Distribute an agenda with an objective.** Attendees will know what to expect and will be better prepared with ideas, problems, and solutions.

STAFF NAME:		Meeting Date:	
Phone/e-mail:			
Meeting Description:			
Audience Size	TIME	From: _____ am/pm	
		To: _____ am/pm	

Catering	❏ No thank you ❏ AM break ❏ Coffee/tea only ❏ Lunch ❏ Continental breakfast ❏ PM break ❏ Full breakfast ❏ Dietary considerations
Audio-Visual	❏ Podium or lectern with microphone ❏ Audience microphone _____ ❏ Lapel microphone _____ ❏ Panel microphone _____ ❏ ELMO projector ❏ Overhead projector ❏ PowerPoint® projector ❏ Video conference ❏ Web conference ❏ Internet access (❏ High-speed)
Room Layout	❏ Classroom ❏ Rounds ❏ Theatre ❏ N/A ❏ U-shape

SPECIAL INSTRUCTIONS - (Break or lunch times, etc.)

❏ Completed by: _____ Phone: _____
❏ Room assigned: _____

⊕ **Get prepared.** Don't just show up at the meeting. As an attendee, have questions and comments ready. As a presenter, if you have a complex subject, don't bore everyone with the details. Explain the highlights and get to the bottom line quickly.

During the Meeting

⊕ **Turn off the gadgets.** Before you enter the meeting, turn off your cell phone, PDA, or anything else that would cause a disruption. If you can't talk, you shouldn't answer the phone. Respect others and give the meeting your undivided attention so it will end on time.

⊕ **Have stand-up meetings.** If you want to end a meeting quickly, have everyone stand the entire time.

⊕ **Start on time.** Once you establish that your meetings start on time, people will make a better effort to be prompt. Don't restart the meeting or waste time recapping information for every late arrival.

⊕ **State the objective.** What is the specific purpose of the meeting? What do you hope to accomplish by having the meeting? People will stay focused if they are reminded of what the desired outcome is.

⊕ **Designate a timekeeper.** Stick to the agenda and value other people's time by staying on schedule.

TIP

Find a Date and Time Everyone Can Meet

One of the most miserable and time-consuming aspects of convening a meeting is finding a time all of the participants can meet. **If** you use Microsoft Outlook® and are on a Microsoft Exchange® Server, use **AutoPick**.

Create the meeting request (**Ctrl+Shift+Q**) and invite participants as you normally would.

At the bottom, left of the Scheduling tab, click **AutoPick Next>>** and let Outlook check the time you have entered.

Continue to click until an acceptable time is found.

- ☉ Designate someone to take minutes. Few people enjoy this chore, so rotate the responsibility every six months or so (if yours is not a formal organization with an assigned secretary). Handwritten minutes can be disseminated more quickly than transcribed records.

- ☉ Take good notes. Stay focused on the most important aspects of the meeting and take notes that you will be able to refer to later. Pay particular attention to due dates for work you are responsible for.

- ☉ Stay on point. Keep the meeting objective in mind as you bring up questions and comments. Designate a board or workspace to table ideas that need more explanation or a different meeting later.

- ☉ Pay attention and give everyone the respect they deserve. Better to stay at your desk and get work done than attend a meeting and not pay attention.

- ☉ Know what the next step is. If any type of follow-on work is expected after the meeting, be clear on what the next steps are.

- ☉ Stop on time. Respect other people's schedules and workloads by ending the meeting at the published time.

After the Meeting

⊙ **Review your notes.** While your memory is fresh, move tasks to whatever project tracking system you use (to-do list, computer tasks, project folders, tickler file, etc.). If it is something you can do quickly, go ahead.

⊙ **Schedule time to get the work done.** If you must complete meeting-related tasks that will require blocks of time, make sure you mark that on your schedule.

⊙ **Ask attendees for suggestions on how to improve the meeting.** One voice speaks volumes, so even if you only get one comment or suggestion on how to make your meetings more effective, don't assume it's not an important change.

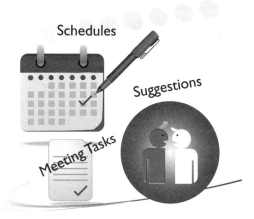

Schedules

Suggestions

Meeting Tasks

The Time Management Memory Jogger™ | ©2008 GOAL/QPC

Improvement Ten:
Delegate As Much As You Can

Create more time to work on your core responsibilities by getting work done through others.

What is the benefit of delegating as much as I can?

Delegation frees you up to concentrate on work you should be doing but have not had time to do.

What concepts must I understand to delegate effectively?

Delegation is an important management skill, as well as a critical personal time-management skill. If you aren't the right person to do the work, you have to decide who is and pass that work along. Then you can devote more time to the core activities you are more suited for.

Members of your team will grow as they take on more responsibility and are held accountable for the results. Do you really need to be in on every decision? Won't that cause work to be held up? Do you sleep

---

with your PDA under your pillow because you don't trust anyone in your organization to handle things?

What is your main contribution to the company? How do you add the most value? Focus on that and delegate appropriately.

What actions must I take to delegate effectively?

Initially, delegation will take more time than if you did the work yourself. You will have to invest the necessary time to teach others how to complete the tasks, and then hold them accountable for getting them done on time and on schedule.

Communicate It Right the First Time

How many times have you received what you thought would be a final work product only to find out the employee didn't understand what you wanted? Not only have you wasted valuable time explaining a project, the employee wasted valuable time developing the wrong deliverable. Was it that you did not communicate properly, or was it that they weren't listening? It is a combination of both.

Good communication involves clearly explaining your thoughts or desires to someone who is listening and understanding what you mean. Here are tips that will help you become a better communicator.

Give Logical Instructions

Before you ask someone for help, you should first have a clear understanding of what you want to happen. After all, how can you explain what you want if you don't fully grasp it yourself?

1. Give an overview. State the purpose of the work and let the employee know how it fits into the overall plan. Give their work purpose.

2. Explain the specifics. Fill in the details once they understand the scope.

3. Be clear about the result. Make sure everyone understands exactly what you want the result to look like. What is the deliverable: a three-page report? a slide presentation? a letter? Can you show them any samples?

4. Empower them to make decisions. Once an employee is properly trained and you feel confident that they have the skills to do the job, allow them to decide some things on their own. With proper training, they will learn when they should come to you with questions.

Listen to Understand

Listening well will save time. Before you start, make sure you understand what you have been asked to do.

1. Ask probing questions and take good notes. When you are listening, ask good questions and take enough notes to help you later. Don't assume you understand. Avoid ques-

tions that can be answered with a simple yes or no so you will get more information.

2. **Listen actively.** Use reflective listening and rephrase important points back to the speaker. Repeating it in your own words assures you that you understand ("So as I understand it…"). When the speaker also agrees, you'll both be working from the same place.

3. **Ask for a specific due date.** Don't accept ASAP as a due date. It may be an important project, but it might not be urgent. Find out what's driving the deadline.

4. **Negotiate the due date.** If you plan your days, prioritize your work, organize your workspace and files, and streamline the work with technology, and the schedule is still tight, then you have earned the right to say you need more time. Negotiate the due date now if you need to.

Track Delegated Work

You should devise a simple system for tracking work you have delegated and for work that has been delegated to you.

Electronic Method. The best option for tracking tasks is to use an electronic tool that allows you to sort tasks, relate them to other projects, set reminders, and keep information portable.

TIP

Example:
Communicating Both Ways

Manager

"We have to get our customer service numbers up by at least twenty more points before the next managers meeting. Can you compile a simple list of the top ten complaints we are getting? And please include two or three solutions for each complaint. I will need it by next Tuesday at noon."

Employee

"Do you need me to focus on any one department or job function, or do you need an overall report?"

"Which areas are of greatest concern?"

"Do you need a dollar estimate for the suggestions that I will propose? And, if you do, how much detail do you need?"

"So as I understand it…"

Continued…

TIP

Example:
Communicating Both Ways

"Is a document with accompanying charts sufficient or would you prefer a slide presentation?"

"I am working on the board committee reports and have to have them ready for the meeting by Monday morning. Could I get the customer service report to you by next Thursday afternoon instead?" (You think you can finish it by Wednesday morning but you want some wiggle room in case something happens.)

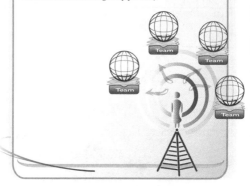

- ④ **Outlook tasks.** Drag information to Tasks and assign, sort, and set reminders.

- ④ **Excel spreadsheet.** List all tasks in the spreadsheet and use filters, sorts, and hyperlinks. Create headings such as Name, Description, Date Sent, Due Date, Staff, Comments, Status.

- ④ **Project software.** Maintain schedules for more complex work done in teams with a project manager.

Paper Method. You can keep things simple with paper when the work is not very involved.

- ④ **Tracking form.** Create a simple form with headings similar to the Excel spreadsheet described previously.

- ④ **Tickler file.** When you delegate work, make a copy of the top page of a document before you hand it off, and place this copy in your tickler file as a reminder. If you have received work to do, put the document in the tickler file behind the due date and set a calendar reminder to get it done.

- ④ **Calendar reminders.** Make notes on your calendar and use this in conjunction with some type of tickler file, as explained above.

Complete Staff Work

When you're given an assignment, your boss will use that information to make critical decisions. Your preparatory work should be complete. The term, "complete staff work," is the study of a problem and the presentation of a solution, whereas all that is left for management to do is to make the required decision.

A Step-by-Step Process

The next time someone relies on you for an answer, try this.

1. Recognize and define the assignment.

   ☺ Make sure you understand the objective—what you are expected to accomplish. What is the purpose of the work?

   ☺ Be clear on the priority and deadline. If you know you will not be able to complete the work by the due date, negotiate the deadline. Sometimes you won't know right away whether you will have time to complete a project because you won't have analyzed it yet. Make that statement up front in case you have to come back to renegotiate the due date.

   ☺ Understand how the solution should be presented (the deliverable). Should it be a computer presentation, concise report, letter? Find out who the ultimate audience is and the level of detail they want.

   ☺ Determine whether any outside resources are already available to help. Who else might already know about the project?

   ☺ Outline your action plan. Invest time up front to plan your project, whether it's painting a bedroom or completing a report. The more time you invest on the initial planning, the less likely it will be that you'll have to start over. If you break your project into smaller phases, you'll be able to better determine how long each one will take.

2. **Put a tracking system in place.** You will have to decide how to track the progress of your project. You could use project software, a spreadsheet, your tickler file, or a desktop file with notes in your calendar. Whatever system you put in place, faithfully maintain it.

3. **Gather the facts.** Once it's clear what the assignment is and how you will approach it, you'll have to use all available resources to research possible solutions. Document all your information sources in case you have to verify your data.

4. **Analyze your data.** Once your research is complete, you will have to analyze it. To make this easier, organize the information into a logical format, delete anything irrelevant, review and test your hypothesis with other people (not your manager), and revise it until you're satisfied with it.

5. **Develop Plans B & C.** You should at least have a Plan B. Review the objectives and identify one or two additional alternatives. Look at the problem from every imaginable angle, considering positive and negative effects, your common sense, and gut instinct. Then choose your position.

6. **Create your deliverable.** Once you develop a solution, create your deliverable, whether it is a letter, a multimedia presentation, a report, or so on.

7. **Conduct a preliminary review**. Have someone else review your solution before handing it off to the decision maker. Make sure you have done all your homework and have assessed the validity of the information, as well as the associated costs and benefits. Revise all work as needed.

8. **Prepare answers to questions in advance**. Questions you received in the preliminary review are indicative of what your boss might ask you. Use this feedback to prepare your answers in advance.

9. **Finalize the deliverable**. You have done the research and developed what you think is a viable solution. You have alternative solutions as a backup. Now make sure the deliverable is in the requested format and free of errors.

10. **Deliver your solution**. It's time to go to the boss. But before you do, ask yourself this question: "If I were the boss, would I stake my career, mortgage, or car payment—and my professional reputation—on the accuracy of this information?" If not, revisit Step 3.

The main point of complete staff work is that when the work is presented to the requestor, there is nothing left for him to do but to make the decision, sign the letter, or make the call.

Improvement Eleven:
Use the Right Technology

Integrate technology with logical business
processes, and then learn how to use it.

What is the benefit of using the right technology?

The right technological tools will help you get organized and complete your work quickly and accurately.

What concepts must I understand to use the right technology?

Technology can't solve your problems if you don't
know what the problems are. Figure that out, determine how the technology will be used, buy what fits,
and then learn how to use it.

What actions must I take to use the right technology?

Technology should integrate with well-thought-out
business processes. Some of these solutions will
need to be researched and analyzed, but some are

no-brainers—it just makes sense to do it. Here are four examples:

- ⊕ Dual monitors that increase your desktop space.
- ⊕ Search engines that help you find what you need more quickly.
- ⊕ Macros and templates that can save you hours of typing and formatting.
- ⊕ Data backups that can save your business after a disaster.

Use Dual Monitors

You can boost your productivity if you double your desktop workspace by adding an additional monitor to your computer. Some ways to use them include:

- ⊕ Using one to conduct Internet research and dragging good information to the other.
- ⊕ Viewing your calendar on one and checking e-mail on the other.
- ⊕ Reading instructions on one and performing the steps on the other.
- ⊕ Browsing image thumbnails on one and the full-sized previews on the other.

If you use a laptop, you can simply plug the additional monitor into the same connection that you would use for a projector. If you use an older desktop computer, you may have to install a second video adapter. Either way, after you make the connection, you will have to enable Dualview (conduct a simple Internet search to find out how to set this up on your computer).

NOTE Using dual monitors is not multitasking, but simply an extension of how much you can see on your computer screen.

Find What You Need With Search Engines

Search engines use complicated algorithms (programs) called spiders to crawl the Web looking for information on sites. They then store links to the information on their sites.

Each search engine retrieves and presents information differently and can be used to fulfill different needs. You should use different engines to become familiar with how they work and to determine how reliable they are in returning relevant data.

TIP
View Outlook® Calendar on Second Monitor

If you use Outlook®, to view your calendar on one monitor and your e-mail on the other, right-click the **Calendar** icon, left-click **Open in New Window**, and drag the calendar to the second monitor.

When you drag an e-mail message to your calendar, click the date first, then drag (if you keep your calendar in a view that shows times, also click and drag out the time of the meeting that is suggested in the message).

Selecting the date and time before you drag the message to the calendar will cause it to land on the right date at the right time (this only works if you view your calendar in a separate window).

work   calendar

Here is a list of ways you can use search engines that you may not have considered.

① **Use for tech support.** When you receive an error message on your computer, you don't have to waste hours trying to determine what is wrong. Search for the error message text (in quotation marks to look for the exact phrase). Your answer will most likely show up in a forum that is manned by experts. Someone else has had the same problem and you will most likely find a solution.

① **Find what you need with bits of information.** When you need to find something and you can't remember a lot of details, type everything you know about it in the search box. For instance, you saw a company on CNN news, you remember they make boxes, they are located in Georgia, and the person they interviewed was named Steve. In the search box, type: CNN box manufacturer Georgia Steve. Most likely the company wrote about Steve's appearance on CNN, and a press release about it is on their web site. The search engines have already indexed the page and will take you right to it.

① **Use it to end clutter.** As you are getting organized, you can recycle a lot of paper because you'll be able to search for the information if you ever need it again.

① **Research callers who did not leave a subject.** If someone leaves you a voicemail with a phone number and a name you can't understand, you can research the phone number. You can at least find out what business they are calling from.

Advanced Search

If you want to find answers quickly on the Internet, narrowing your search by using the engine's advanced search option.

TIP Advanced Search Option

Look for the advanced search option of your favorite search engine. Using Google™ as an example, at www.Google.com, to the right of the search box is a link to Advanced Search. This form makes it easy to set up your search for the most relevant web pages. You can specify a search for pages that have all of the words you type, an exact wording or phrase (or put this inside quotation marks on the basic search page), any unwanted words to avoid, and more. You can also indicate which web site you want to search.

Save Hours with Templates and Macros

It's common to spend way too much time cutting, pasting, moving, resizing, redesigning, and distributing similar documents to appropriate personnel. If you frequently create documents that contain specialized formatting but not always the same text, you can save hours if you create a template. The template is a shell document with formatting, boilerplate text, headers and footers, macros, and more. You will base future documents on this template and have more time to focus on the content.

Another big timesaver is a macro. If you use the same set of keystrokes and mouse actions to create or edit documents, you can record those steps (the macro) and create a toolbar button or keyboard combination. It's possible to take a tedious, miserable task and get it done with the click of a button.

Back Up Your Data for Business Recovery

According to government statistics, ninety-three percent of companies that had trouble restoring their data after a disaster go out of business within eighteen months. A smaller business could be out of business in a day.

Employees in large corporate or government environments may not have to concern themselves with data recovery at work, but smaller organizations do.

Protect your data by backing it up. Many options are available such as an external hard drive, but an online solution is best because it stores the data offsite. These media vaults monitor your computer while you are online and will automatically back up anything new. All of your data is encrypted for extra security and you can access it from any web browser.

Other Technologies that Enhance Productivity

The following technology suggestions will help you increase your productivity, but they should be analyzed for fit based on your needs.

Access and Protect Data

Access your computer remotely	www.LogMeIn.com provides free remote access to your computer via any web browser. Whatever you can do when you are physically at your computer, you will be able to do remotely over the web. Your computer will have to be connected to the Internet.
Uninterrupted Internet connection	In order for remote access via the web to work (see www.LogMeIn.com), you will need an uninterrupted Internet connection. If you are still using dial-up, your ISP may disconnect you if it detects long periods of inactivity. **Stay Connected!** by www.inKlineGlobal.com, is an award-winning connectivity utility that guarantees you will never

Continued...

Access and Protect Data

	get disconnected from your ISP (unless your office experiences long periods of power outages).
Portable computer storage	A flash drive (also called jump drive or stick) is a portable memory storage device (about the size of a stick of gum) that fits into any USB port. Its storage capacity surpasses that of most older computers.
	Security is a major concern with flash drives because they're so small they're easy to lose or have stolen. **TrueCrypt.com** offers a free encryption technology that password protects data on a flash drive.
	CoSoSys.com's **Carry it Easy™** offers encryption that prevents others from *Continued...*

Continued...

Access and Protect Data

using their flash drive to steal data off your computer. And the **USB Drive Lost & Found™** will let someone who finds your flash drive see who you are but not see your data.

The **U3 flash drive** (a smart drive) from SanDisk® has encryption built in (www.U3.com). You can securely store your data and software applications on it, plug it into any computer's USB port, enter a password for access, and work wherever you are. When you unplug it, no personal data is left behind. It will be as if you were never there. A list of existing software that has been configured to use this technology is on their web site. *Continued...*

Access and Protect Data

Receive faxes in e-mail	If you don't receive a lot of faxes, try www.efax.com (http://home.efax.com/s/r/e faxprint), or a similar service, to receive faxes directly in your Inbox for free. You will have to pay a small fee if you want to send faxes (if you have a printer/fax combo, use that instead).
Share documents and your calendar for free when you are not on a network	Google™, the company with the Internet's most widely used search engine, has developed free technology that allows you to share documents with others. Anyone you have invited to either edit or view your documents or presentations can sign in and access it at www.Google.com. You can also share your Outlook® calendar and give certain people access to it or make it public. *Continued...*

Access and Protect Data

	Gmail™ is Google's free, web-based e-mail technology. If you have numerous e-mail accounts and are currently going to different web sites to check them, you can forward all of them to Gmail™ for one-stop reading.
Synchronize files on different computers without a network	You can keep file folders synchronized between computers over the Internet with www.FolderShare.com. The computers don't need to be on the same network. FolderShare is free and works as long as the computers are online. It allows you to share files and collaborate with others, and you can remotely access files via the web.

Continued...

Connect to Data

Connect your laptop wirelessly to the Internet from almost anywhere	The **aircard** (or mobile broadband card) is a device that enables wireless Internet access and is used mostly with laptops. It connects via an available USB port, PCMCIA card slot, or the faster Express Card slot. Its advantage is that you will not have to rely on finding a hot spot, phone line, or wired connection to get online. If you justify needing one, opt for the unlimited access plan.
Smartphone (Personal Digital Assistant (PDA) with cell phone)	The PDA is a little computer that fits in your hand. You can carry your office with you, including your calendar, contacts, fax capabilities, media player, and more. The smartphone technology combines the early PDA capabilities with a cell phone. *Before you choose a smartphone, you should first determine why you need one and how you will use it.* Continued...

Organize Data

Convert text on a page to a contact or appointment	Anagram™ instantly creates new contacts or calendar appointments from any text you select on your computer screen, including e-mail signatures, web directories, and search results.
Scan business cards	If you have piles of business cards, use a business card scanner to build a database of names, addresses, etc. **CardScan®** (www.Corex.com) takes information scanned from business cards and inserts it into the correct fields of its searchable electronic address book. With the click of a button, you will be able to export contacts into your database software. Purge the old cards first. Group cards into categories and batch scan.

Organize Data

Scan and organize travel receipts on the road	NEATReceipts™ is a software and scanner that is lightweight enough for travel. You can scan, analyze, and organize your receipts, bills, business cards, and more. It stores everything in a database on your PC. This product takes the dread out of submitting your travel expense statements. You can scan receipts in your hotel room and have all your statements completed and e-mailed before you get home.
Scan multiple pages with a sheetfeeder	If you are trying for a paperless office and want to start scanning documents en masse, purchase a scanner with a sheetfeeder. You will be able to load multiple pages at once. *Continued...*

Build Skills

Explore technology you already have	To save hours, work faster by learning whatever software you open every day.
Learn how to type	The faster you type, the quicker you will finish your work. A typing test and a free video game that teaches you how to type are at www.touch-typing-tutor.com.
Read faster with speed reading	Learn how to read and comprehend faster by increasing the number of words you read in each block of text. You will reduce the length of time you spend reading each block and reduce the number of times your eyes skip back to previous information. You can test your reading speed at www.ReadingSoft.com

Continued...

Manage Your Time

Calculate free time	You can calculate how much free time you have every week at www.SUITEMinute.com. Then you have to decide how you will spend it.
Calculate time value	This online calculator helps you determine how much every hour of your time is worth by looking at your salary against taxation and the cost of living for your region. www.money central.msn.com/investor/calcs/n_time/main.asp
Global Positioning System (GPS)	GPS provides specially-coded satellite signals that can be processed in a receiver to determine its location, speed, direction, and time. Some PDAs come equipped with these receivers or you can purchase a standalone unit. With the accompanying software, you will not waste a lot of time being lost.

Continued...

Manage Your Time

Save time at the airport	The CLEAR® program (**FlyClear.com**) operates at a growing number of airports. With the CLEAR® card, you will be able to go through a dedicated security line at the airport. You will swipe your card and provide your identification marker (thumb, fingers, or eye scan that you provide at a validation center when you sign up in person). A CLEAR® concierge will walk you to the front of the security line.
Voicemail: Bypass voicemail computer loop and get to a live person	Interactive Voice Response (IVR) is known as voicemail jail, or those loops you get into with a computer instead of getting to a live person. If you know the right code, you can bypass the computer and either get to a real person, or the queue to wait for one. **www.GetHuman.com** has

Continued...

Manage Your Time

	compiled a list of all the methods you need to bypass IVR for 500 of the largest, most commonly called companies you are likely to deal with.
Voicemail: Get to the beep	Phone companies use different shortcuts for bypassing an outgoing message and going right to the beep (try #, *, or 1). Once you find out what it is, add the shortcut to your address book for each contact.

Conclusion

If you find that your responsibilities continue to increase, but your time runs out long before your workload does, you can use the solutions you have learned in this book to solve that problem. Once you make the necessary changes to how you work, you'll have more time to think. With more time to think, you'll be able to plan and prioritize better. And with a better plan, you'll be more efficient and effective. And, finally, once you learn to use technology to pull it all together, you'll have even more time.

What Would You Like to Have More Time to Do?

Time Management Training Program

One-Day Workshop
Spend Less Time Working but Get More Done
with Peggy Duncan

Program Description

This practical, one-day workshop covers the concepts outlined in *The Time Management Memory Jogger*™. Your team will learn the principles of organizing and will create a paper management system that they can use immediately upon returning to work.

Participants will also examine their individual work processes and develop a more streamlined approach that includes using technology to automate everything they need to do.

Learn How To

⏲ Examine how you are spending the workday and eliminate time wasters.

⏲ Organize everything around you so you can think clearly and have more time to plan.

⏲ Unclutter your mind with external cues that will help your retention.

⏲ Prioritize your projects and explore ways to streamline the work.

⏲ Incorporate the right technology and finish work more quickly.

Visit our web site at **www.MemoryJogger.com** for more information about this workshop and all our other training courses.

Index

Time Log

☐ Work
☐ Home

Time	Activity	Planned	Inter-ruption	Priority (A-D)	People

Time Log

☐ Work
☐ Home

Time	Activity	Planned	Inter-ruption	Priority (A-D)	People

The Time Management Memory Jogger™ | ©2008 GOAL/QPC

	Time Log	☐ Work ☐ Home			
Time	Activity	Planned	Inter-ruption	Priority (A-D)	People

Time Log

☐ Work
☐ Home

Time	Activity	Planned	Inter-ruption	Priority (A-D)	People

The Time Management Memory Jogger™ | ©2008 GOAL/QPC

Time Log

☐ Work
☐ Home

Time	Activity	Planned	Inter-ruption	Priority (A-D)	People

Time Log

☐ Work
☐ Home

Time	Activity	Planned	Inter-ruption	Priority (A-D)	People